Rock and Roll Facts

Copyright © 2020 Bill Lonero. All rights reserved.
ISBN: 9798663761758

Cover Photo of Jimmy Page by Neil Zlozower

DEDICATION

Rock and Roll Facts is dedicated to all the musicians on every stage across the world. The ones that pack up their car and drive 2 hours to play a gig for less money than the gas it took to get there. For the musicians that stand on the big stages, pretending to be their heroes. To the studio musicians that remain nameless but play on all the hit songs that have become the soundtracks to our lives. Being a musician is hard work and most of the time it goes unappreciated. This book is dedicated to anyone who has ever tried to make music a career. Without you, the world would be a boring place.

Rock and Roll Facts

1. "Bad Finger Boogie" was the original working title of The Beatles' "With A Little Help From My Friends" because John Lennon had been forced to rely on his middle finger when playing the song's piano part, having injured his forefinger earlier.

2. "Here we are now, entertain us" was what Kurt Cobain would say whenever he entered a party to "break the ice". He later used it in the chorus to 1991's hit 'Smells Like Teen Spirit'.

3. "Smoke on The Water" refers to a Frank Zappa show in Montreux in 1971, where someone lit a flare gun and "burned the place to the ground".

4. "Song 2" by Blur was meant to be a parody of American grunge music.

5. "Dragula" by White Zombie was inspired by the classic TV show "The Munsters" and a dragster driven by Grandpa Munster, Al Lewis.

6. "Every Breath You Take" by The Police is supposed to be about someone obsessed with a lost lover, and who stalks them. Sting, who wrote it, is troubled by how many people think it is a love song.

7. "I Don't Want to Miss a Thing" was originally written for Celine Dion by Diane Warren, not for Aerosmith.

8. "I Love Rock and Roll" was a cover song originally recorded by The Arrows, not Joan Jett.

9. "Side of A Bullet" from Nickelback features a posthumous Dimebag Darrell solo assembled from outtakes from Pantera's "Vulgar Display of Power" and "Far Beyond Driven" albums. The tribute to Nickelback's murdered drinking buddy remains the band's most personal moment.

10. "Sweet Child O' Mine" was written in 5 minutes by Guns 'N Roses.

11. "Under Pressure" was written by David Bowie and Queen during a 24-hour wine and cocaine marathon.

12. 1 in every 14 people in the US under the age of 50 are estimated to have owned a copy of "The Dark Side of The Moon" by Pink Floyd.

13. 1989's "Batman" soundtrack album was mainly composed by Prince and is considered to be his 11th studio album, but

since Prince had to agree to sign the publishing rights over to Warner Bros, none of the high-charting "Batman" songs appear on future hits compilations.

14. A 10+ hour film version of Dune was almost produced with Salvador Dali as the Emperor, with art by HR Giger and music by Pink Floyd.

15. A Cannibal Corpse sticker can be seen in Jack Black's character's bedroom in the 2003 movie "School of Rock".

16. A dentist introduced The Beatles to LSD by slipping it into their coffee.

17. A friend once asked John Lennon what the best lyric was he ever wrote. "That's easy," replied Lennon, "All you need is love."

18. A lightning machine from the laboratory set in Universal's 1931 horror classic "Frankenstein" was used at early dates on the 1976 KISS Destroyer tour, where it was dubbed the "God of Thunder Machine". A giant Tesla coil that emitted colored electrical beams, designed by Ken Strickfaden, it was soon abandoned for being too cumbersome and unreliable.

Rock and Roll Facts

19. A line in David Bowie's hit, "Space Oddity" says "And the papers want to know whose shirt you wear". "Whose shirt you wear" is English slang for "What football team are you a fan of?"

20. A statue of Phil Lynott of Thin Lizzy was put up off Grafton street in Dublin in 2005.

21. A talent manager named Jim Denny told Elvis Presley to "stick to driving a truck because you'll never make it as a singer" after a performance at the Grand Ole Opry.

22. A U.S. psychedelic rock band called Coven released a song called "Black Sabbath" in 1969 (prior to Earth's name change to Black Sabbath) and their bassist was named Oz Osborne. Coven later went on to record "One Tin Soldier" for the hit movie Billy Jack.

23. AC/DC got their name from a sewing machine.

24. AC/DC guitarist Malcolm Young once worked as a sewing-machine mechanic in a bra factory.

25. According to Pat Vegas of the band Redbone, Jimi Hendrix wanted to join the group, but was prevented from doing so because he was already under contract.

26. Actress Katey Sagal, best known as Peg Bundy, not only dated Gene Simmons in the mid-70s, but she also sang on his solo album as well as back-up for Molly Hatchet, Bob Dylan and Bette Midler.

27. Aerosmith appeared in The Beatles movie "Sgt. Pepper's Lonely Hearts Club Band" as The Future Villain Band in 1978.

28. Aerosmith had once written the music for a song but could not come up with any words. They finally got their inspiration when they went to see Young Frankenstein movie. The song was Walk This Way, became one of the band's biggest hits.

29. Aerosmith made more money from Guitar Hero than any albums.

30. Aerosmith's "I Don't Want to Miss a Thing" was originally written for Celine Dion.

31. After being fired from Cannibal Corpse in 1993, guitarist Bob Rusay traded his guitar for golf clubs and became a certified instructor for an Arizona country club.

32. After Elvis Presley performed Simon & Garfunkel's "Bridge Over Troubled Water", Paul Simon, who attended the show, said, "That's it, we might as well all give up now."

33. After his departure from Anthrax, lead guitarist Dan Spitz became a master watchmaker trained by the prestigious Bulova school in Switzerland.

34. Mike Mangini of Dream Theater/Steve Vai/Extreme is also a software specialist who worked on a program that studied the links between the human brain and body.

35. After Kurt Cobain's death, Dave Grohl almost joined Tom Petty and the Heartbreakers after playing with them on Saturday Night Live.

36. After leaving Megadeth in 2003, guitarist Marty Friedman moved to Japan and used his command of the Japanese language to become a popular TV show host.

37. After Prince converted to Jehovah's Witness in May of 2001, he stopped performing at least 50 songs due to explicit content, including "Little Red Corvette" and "Cream".

38. After radio DJ Rodney Bingenheimer saw the band perform at Gazzari's on the Sunset Strip, he invited KISS co-lead Gene Simmons to their next show. Simmons went on to produce a Van Halen demo tape, which he later took to his management team who rejected the band.

39. After Sam Phillips built a new recording studio in 1959, the original Sun Records building at 706 Union Avenue, Memphis, Tennessee, became a warehouse for auto parts. In 1987, the original building was reopened as Sun Studio, a recording label and tourist attraction.

40. After seeing Elvis in concert, Liberace suggested he wear flashy costumes. Elvis took the advice and began sporting gold lame jackets and jeweled white jumpsuits.

41. After the Freddie Mercury Tribute Concert was announced in 1992, all 72,000 tickets for the Wembley Arena show sold out in 3 hours, even though no performers were announced besides the remaining members of Queen.

42. After they were lambasted for calling Judas Priest a "Death Metal" band in 2014, Simpsons' writers punished Bart Simpson by having him fill a chalkboard with the phrase "Judas Priest is not a death metal band" on the following episode.

43. Al Kooper, who played organ on Dylan's "Like A Rolling Stone," had never played organ before the session. He had turned up to the studio hoping to play guitar and, finding an excellent guitarist (Mike Bloomfield) already on hand, sat down at the organ instead. After the first take the session producer told Dylan to lose the organ part; Dylan replied that he wanted it louder.

44. Alan Parsons (audio engineer of "Dark Side of the Moon") rejected Pink Floyd's invitation to work as the audio engineer of "Wish You Were Here" and started his own band, The Alan Parsons Project.

45. Alfred Wertheimer, the photographer assigned to document Elvis Presley's early career, recalled that he shot in black and white because Elvis' label, RCA, refused to pay for high-priced color film and processing, uncertain if Elvis was going to be worth it.

46. Alice Cooper has a golf handicap of 3.

47. All members of Nirvana were kicked out of their own release party for "Nevermind" for starting a food fight.

48. Although he was named Johnny Allen Hendrix at birth, his tombstone reads James M. "Jimi" Hendrix.

49. An article that appeared in London's Sunday Times in early May 2019, claimed that Queen, the band, had amassed wealth totaling 445 million Pounds, eclipsing British monarch Queen Elizabeth II, who was worth 375 million Pounds.

50. Angus' wife Ellen allegedly told a fan who was travelling on the same train as her and Angus between gigs that when

the band were recording The Razors Edge, they once came into the studio to discover backing vocals where none had been recorded. The vocals purportedly sounded just like Bon Scott.

51. Anthony Kiedis once missed a Red Hot Chili Peppers concert because he was off scoring drugs, so Keith Morris filled in on vocals and just yelled and made up lyrics because he did not know any of the songs.

52. Anton Crowley, who played guitar on Necrophagia's 1999 album "Holocausto" was Pantera's singer Phil Anselmo working under a pseudonym for legal reasons.

53. As of early 2016, Rock 'n' Roll legend Chuck Berry had released 19 studio albums, but only 4 of them ever cracked the Billboard 200 album chart. The only one to enter the Top 100 was 1975's "The London Chuck Berry Sessions", which went to #8.

54. At 1981 Virginia's Hampton Coliseum, while playing "(I Can't Get No) Satisfaction," a fan rushed to the stage, due to which Keith Richards momentarily stopped playing to whack the fan in the head.

55. At 52, Rolling Stones bassist Bill Wyman married 18-year-old Mandy Smith but divorced after a year. Bill's 30-year-old son then Stephen married Mandy's mother, aged 46. If Bill and

Mandy had remained married, Stephen would have been his father's father-in-law and his own grandpa.

56. At a protest against the PMRC (Parents Music Resource Center), Rage Against the Machine went on stage completely naked with duct tape over their mouths at a 1993 concert.

57. At one point, Slayer guitarist Kerry King was a breeder of show dogs.

58. At the beginning of the song Roxanne by The Police, during the intro, you can hear a strange piano chord, then Sting laughing. In fact, during the voice recording, Sting accidentally sat on the piano just behind him. They decided to keep this on the final mix.

59. The members of the 1980s pop/rock band Toto were prolific session musicians. Their work includes Michael Jackson's 'Thriller'. Collectively, the members have been recorded on over 5,000 albums, selling over 500,000,000 albums.

60. Axl Rose once postponed a Guns N' Roses show because he was watching TMNT 2: Secret of the Ooze.

61. Axl Rose smoked cigarettes during a science experiment at

UCLA for $8 an hour.

62. Axl Rose spent $13 million and 15 years recording "Chinese Democracy", making it the most expensive album in history and it flopped.

63. Axl Rose's "Sweet Child of Mine" was Erin Everly, daughter of Don Everly, from the Everly Brothers. Axl and Erin got married, but their marriage only lasted a month.

64. Bad Religion vocalist Greg Graffin earned a Ph.D from Cornell University. His dissertation was titled "Evolution, Monism, Atheism, and the Naturalist World-View".

65. Before Angus Young of AC/DC settled on the schoolboy outfit, he went onstage dressed in a gorilla suit and as Superman. His sister Margaret suggested he wear his schoolboy uniform.

66. Bruce Dickinson of Iron Maiden is a professional pilot, who used to take unpaid leave to front Iron Maiden. He also flies the band on tour on their leased 747.

67. David Grohl was the only band member of the Foo Fighters when recording the first album. He wrote and recorded all vocal, guitar, bass, and drum tracks himself.

Rock and Roll Facts

68. Before being signed to Capitol Records in 1962, The Beach Boys were rejected by Dot, Liberty and Decca Records. They would go on to have thirty-five Billboard Top 40 hits for Capitol.

69. Before Elvis Presley became famous, he had a troubling past of getting bullied. Once in high school, three guys were going to cut his hair off. Then a man, named Red West intervened the scene and stopped them. He would become Elvis's bodyguard and friend and was with him from 1956 to 1975.

70. Before Guns N' Roses, Slash once auditioned for the band Poison, he decided not to join when he was asked about wearing makeup.

71. Before he became Iron Maiden's drummer, Nicko McBrain appeared in their music video for "The Number of the Beast" wearing a devil's mask and shaking a pitchfork.

72. Before joining Metallica, Cliff Burton was in a band called Easy Street with future Faith No More members Jim Martin and Mike Bordin.

73. Before Paul Stanley suggested KISS (prompted by Peter Criss's ex-band Lips), a few other names were considered by

the band. Ace liked Albatross, Peter preferred The Crimson Harpoon and Gene's favorite was F*ck.

74. Before renaming himself Bob Dylan, Robert Allen Zimmerman, named himself Elston Gunn.

75. Before Robert Patrick got the role in Terminator 2: Judgment Day, Billy Idol was chosen to play the liquid T-1000 but was side-lined by an injured leg suffered in a 1990 motorcycle accident.

76. Before Soundgarden, Chris Cornell worked as a seafood wholesaler and was a sous chef at Ray's Boathouse in Seattle, Washington.

77. Joe Perry of Aerosmith once ran up a hotel room service bill of $80,000 while partying with the band.

78. Before starting the band Kiss, Gene Simmons was a sixth-grade teacher.

79. Before Taylor Hawkins joined Foo Fighters, he was drumming for Alanis Morrisette.

80. Behemoth frontman Nergal, is a certified museum curator in his native Poland.

81. Vince Neil killed his friend Razzle from the band Hanoi Rocks one night when he was drunk and they both drove to get more alcohol. Vince Neil's Pantera collided with an oncoming car killing Razzle and leaving the occupants of the other car with severe brain damage. Neil's bandmate Nikki Sixx was on vacation with legendary rock photographer Neil Zlozower and RATT guitarist Robin Crosby at the time.

82. David Bowie was known as a multi-instrumentalist. In addition to his playing of guitar, keyboards, harmonica, and saxophone, he played stylophone, viola, cello, koto, thumb piano, drums, and percussion.

83. Between March 1956 and February 1981, Elvis Presley placed 114 songs in the Top 40 of the Billboard Hot 100. Two of them, "My Way" in December 1977 and "Guitar Man" in February 1981, came after his death.

84. Bill Ward's bright red tights on the cover of Black Sabbath's 1975 album "Sabotage" belonged to his wife.

85. Billy Joel wrote his breakthrough hit, "Just the Way You Are" for his first wife, Elizabeth Weber. The inspiration for the song

was taken directly from the last line in The Four Seasons' 1964 hit, "Rag Doll".

86. Billy Joel's "Only the good die young" is about trying to convince a Catholic girl to lose her virginity.

87. Zakk Wylde of Ozzy Osbourne and his band Black Label Society once went to an Elton John concert and sat in the front rows wearing pink boas and cried during "Candle in the Wind".

88. Black Sabbath and Led Zeppelin had an improvised jam session which was recorded but never released.

89. Black Sabbath wrote the hit song "Paranoid" in 20 minutes to fill the remaining 3 minutes of time on their upcoming album. It is now regarded as one of the greatest rock and heavy metal songs of all time.

90. Billy Idol spent three weeks hosting raucous parties in his Oriental Hotel penthouse in 1989. He was charged $149,000 by the Thailand establishment for room fees and damages. Idol ignored hotel management and refused to vacate the room. Idol had to be forcibly removed by the military, being carried out on a stretcher by Thai soldiers after being shot with a tranquilizer dart.

Rock and Roll Facts

91. Keith Richards once said "I've never had a problem with drugs. I've had problems with the police."

92. On July 27th, 1969 Led Zeppelin were staying at the Edgewater Inn after performing at the Seattle Pop festival. They disrobed a young groupie, tied her to the bed, and inserted pieces of a mudshark into her.

93. The true meaning of the lyrics to "Bohemian Rhapsody" remains a secret within the band Queen.

94. Black Sabbath's infamous Stonehenge stage props were too large to fit in many concert venues, as was later lampooned in "This is Spinal Tap". Sabbath's manager quickly jotted down the dimensions on a napkin, but the design thought he meant meters instead of feet.

95. Bob Dylan missed Woodstock, after being invited, because he did not like hippies.

96. Bon Jovi was the last band to perform at the old Wembley Stadium in London before it was demolished and replaced with the new one that stands today.

97. Bon Scott liked the Young Brothers, but thought they were too inexperienced and too young to rock. The Young

Brothers replied with saying Scott was too old to rock. But after one jam session with each other, it was obvious AC/DC found its new lead singer.

98. Bon Scott of AC/DCs early morning ritual was to gargle with red wine and honey, to help retain the raspy edge to his voice.

99. Alternative rock band The Flaming Lips released an album called "Zaireeka" with four CDs that was designed so that when played simultaneously on four separate audio systems, the four CDs would produce a harmonic or juxtaposed sound.

100. All the performances by Elvis Presley were limited within North America because Elvis' manager Colonel Tom Parker could not get a Visa for himself.

101. Bon Scott took the train to AC/DCs first ever gig at Hammersmith Odeon in November 1976, arriving late. The manager Michael Browning had sent a roadie out to take a picture of the band's name in lights. When the photos were processed, they showed Bon Scott walking up the stairs with his bag slung over his shoulder.

102. Bono from U2 is the only person to be nominated for an Oscar, Grammy, Golden Globe and Nobel Peace Prize.

103. Bono was campaigning to have first-world taxpayers forgive all third world debt whilst hiding U2's earnings from Irish tax collectors in the Netherlands.

104. Bono wears glasses all the time because he has glaucoma.

105. Boz Scaggs' real name is William Royce Scaggs. His handle is shortened from a high school nickname, "Bosley".

106. Brian May of Queen holds a Ph.D in Astrophysics and has gone on to write papers on the subject.

107. Brian May, guitarist for Queen, earned a PhD in astrophysics from Imperial College London in 2007, and was Chancellor of Liverpool John Moore's University from 2008 to 2013. He was a "science team collaborator" with NASA's New Horizons Pluto mission. He is also a co-founder of the awareness campaign Asteroid Day.

108. Brian Wilson's divorce from his wife Marilyn was presided over by Judge Joseph Wapner before he rose to fame on TV.

109. Cozy Powell of Rainbow set a world record by playing 400 drums in under one minute, live on television (BBC).

110. Bruce Springsteen was once an opening act for Anne Murray.

111. Bruce Springsteen's "Born in the U.S.A." was the CD to be pressed in the United States.

112. Bruce Springsteen's classic, "Born to Run", almost became the official song of New Jersey until legislators listened to the lyrics and realized the song was about wanting to get out of New Jersey.

113. Bruce Springsteen's "Born in the USA" is about the negative effects of the Vietnam War on Americans but it is often misunderstood to be a patriotic or nationalistic anthem.

114. Bubbles from Trailer Park Boys is a gifted guitarist who is in a band with Alex Lifeson, founding guitarist of Rush. They are called Bubbles and the sh*t Rockers.

115. Cannibal Corpse dedicated their first album, "Eaten Back to Life", to Alfred Packer, who is generally considered the first American cannibal.

116. Carcass are known for their gory lyrics, yet members of the band are vegetarians.

117. Carl Sagan's team wanted to include the Beatles song "Here Comes the Sun" on the Voyager Golden Records (discs containing greetings in 60 languages, music and sounds from Earth aboard both Voyager spacecraft launched in 1977), but the record company EMI, which held the copyrights, declined.

118. Cass Elliot (Mama Cass of The Mamas & Papas) and Keith Moon of The Who died in the apartment of the same singer/songwriter: Harry Nilsson.

119. Charlie Watts of The Rolling Stones has 4 vintage cars even though he does not have a license.

120. Cheap Trick are the only band that AC/DC have ever invited to encore with them. The band first played together at Greensboro in North Carolina on December 18, 1977. The band would enjoy a friendly relationship, continuing to jam together over the years. The only other person invited to jam with AC/DC was Atlantic Records exec Phil Carson, with the band in Brussels on January 25, 1981, on a cover of Little Richard's "Lucille".

121. Cher was a background vocalist on the Righteous Brothers' "You've Lost That Lovin' Feeling". She also sang on "Be My

Baby" The Ronettes and on Darlene Love's singles.

122. Chip Taylor wrote the song "Wild Thing," which was later performed by Jimi Hendrix. Chip is Angelina Jolie's uncle.

123. Chrysler (Automobile company) offered Bruce Springsteen $12 million to use "Born in the U.S.A." in an ad campaign. Springsteen turned them down and has still never let his music be used to sell products.

124. Chuck Berry aspired to be a professional photographer and only performed music to buy photography equipment.

125. Chuck Berry created Berry Park in Missouri, his own rock n roll themed amusement park with a guitar-shaped swimming pool, in response to the whites-only country clubs from where he was once excluded.

126. Chuck Berry earns all the royalties from the Beach Boy's 1963 hit single "Surfin' USA", which he won in a copyright infringement lawsuit unbeknownst to the Beach Boys for 25 years.

127. Chuck Berry played a Gibson 355 guitar for most of his career.

128. Chuck Berry was born in St. Louis, Missouri not San Jose, California as Rolling Stone magazine reported.

129. Collective Soul got mislabeled as a Christian rock band after the release of their single "Shine."

130. Combat Records lost Dave Mustaine's sketch of Vic Rattlehead, which was to be used on the band's debut album "Killing is my Business...and Business is Good". Instead they found some ketchup and a cheap plastic skull.

131. Country legend, Waylon Jennings used to play bass for Buddy Holly. He gave up his seat on the ill-fated plane that killed Holly, Richie Valens, and The Big Bopper.

132. Courtney Love was the lead singer of Faith No More in the early 80s. She was fired before the band became popular.

133. Creedence Clearwater Revival's John Fogerty has said that he is in on the joke where people have mis-heard his lyrics to "Bad Moon Rising" and sing There's a bathroom on the right instead of There's A Bad Moon On The Rise. He has even admitted that he intentionally sings the wrong words in concert about half the time.

134. Dave Grohl of Foo Fighters and Nirvana has been the drummer on every Tenacious D album and is considered a member of the band.

135. Dave Grohl tried to quit Nirvana once after he overheard Kurt Cobain calling him a "sh*tty drummer" but was convinced to stay by the band's manager.

136. Dave Grohl was so intimidated by Kurt Cobain that he hid a lot of the music he made while on tour with Nirvana. After Cobain's death, the tucked away music would become Foo Fighters' first album.

137. Dave Mustaine was kicked out of Metallica right before their debut album was recorded because of his drinking. Soon after, Metallica would be known as "Alcoholica" and Mustaine would form Megadeth.

138. David Bowie performed at the Berlin Wall, while East Germans gathered to listen behind. He recalled, "And we would hear them cheering and singing along from the other side. God, even now I get choked up. It was breaking my heart. I'd never done anything like that in my life, and I guess I never will again."

139. David Bowie was born David Robert Jones. He changed his name to Bowie to avoid being confused with Davey Jones from the Monkees.

140. David Lee Roth's 1985, Billboard #12 hit "Just A Gigolo/I Ain't Got Nobody", was written in 1928 and recorded by Jazz artist Ted Lewis in 1931.

141. Deep Purple was recognized by The Guinness Book of World Records as the "globe's loudest band". When in a concert at the London Rainbow Theatre their sound reached 117 dB. Three of their audience members were rendered unconscious. They have seen been beaten by AC/DC and The Rolling Stones.

142. Despite all the hits that they have had, The Who have never had a number one record in the U.K. or the U.S.

143. Dick Clark's wife suggested that Ernest Evans change his name to "Chubby Checker" as a parody of "Fats Domino".

144. Dimebag Darrel of Pantera was once owner of a goat whose goatee he would dye to match his own colorful goatee.

145. Dimebag Darrell pf Pantera once asked Eddie Van Halen for a copy of his guitar "Bumblebee" from the cover of Van Halen II. Eddie said yes but forgot, but after Dimebag was murdered on stage by a deranged fan, Eddie turned up at the viewing with the original and it is now buried with him.

146. Distortion was popularized by Dave Davies of the band The Kinks. He took a razorblade to the speaker of his amplifier cabinet and sliced it.

147. Disturbed shot the video for the song "Stricken" in the same abandoned hospital used in certain scenes of the horror classic "A Nightmare on Elm Street".

148. Donald Fagan of Steely Dan had stage fright and never sang lead on the band's first concerts.

149. Donnie from The Wild Thornberrys animated show was voiced by Flea, the bassist from Red Hot Chili Peppers.

150. Doug Fieger of The Knack wrote "My Sharona" for 17 year old Sharona Alperin, a girl that he dated for four years. She went on to become a realtor in Los Angeles, promoting her listings on her website, MySharona.com.

151. Drummer Keith Moon's habit of blowing up toilets with fireworks led him to get banned from the Holiday Inn, Sheraton, and Hilton chains for life.

152. Drummer Nick Mason is the only member to appear on every Pink Floyd album.

Rock and Roll Facts

153. Duran Duran took their name from a mad scientist in the 1968 Jane Fonda movie Barbarella.

154. During a brief power-outage at Nirvana in Munich, Krist Novoselic joked "We're on the way out. Grunge is dead. Nirvana's over." It would be Nirvana's last concert before Cobain's death.

155. During a concert in Ireland, Dave Mustaine (of Megadeth) drunkenly dedicated a song to "the cause" and yelled "give Ireland back to the Irish!". A riot then broke out between the Catholics and Protestants and Megadeath had to travel in a bulletproof bus.

156. During a Queen concert in the 70s, a heckler shouted "you f*cking poof" [gay slur] to Freddie Mercury during the middle of their set. Freddie responded by ordering the crew to turn the spotlight on the man, asking him to "Say it again, darling". The heckler cowered in shame.

157. During his time away from the band Venom, bassist, and vocalist Conrad "Cronos" Lant became a dedicated bodybuilder and health enthusiast.

158. During the English broadcast of the Apollo 11 moon landing, Pink Floyd was the background music, jamming live in the BBC studios.

Rock and Roll Facts

159. During the last years that Elvis Presley performed live, he opened his shows with "The Theme From 2001". When asked about it, Presley said that he felt the number 2001 had a special significance in his life that he could not explain. Elvis died August 16th, 1977, which numerically is 8-16-1977. When these numbers are added up, they equal 2001.

160. During the period of 2000-2009 Dave Matthews Band sold more tickets and earned more money than any other act in North America.

161. Elvis's autopsy report is sealed until 2027 by his father Vernon Presley.

162. During the recording of Iron Maiden's "Number of the Beast", unexplained phenomena occurred. This all climaxed when the producer, Martin Birch, was involved in a car accident with a mini-bus transporting a group of nuns, after which he was presented with a repair bill for £666.

163. During the summer of 1959, Bobby Vee and his band, The Shadows were looking for a piano player. A young man who introduced himself as Elston Gunn was auditioned and hired in time to play a gig in Gwinner, North Dakota. Unfortunately, Gunn did not have his own piano and the only one available was terribly out of tune. Without any money to acquire an instrument, Gunn and The Shadows parted company soon after. A few years later Vee spotted a picture on an album that looked a lot like Gunn. It turned

out that his old friend had found solo success under a new name, Bob Dylan.

164. Cynthia Albritton a.k.a Cynthia Plaster Caster has made plaster molds of more than 50 rock stars penises since the 1960s. Jimi Hendrix was her first subject.

165. Dusty Springfield used to spend hundreds of dollars on cheap china then blow off steam by breaking it all.

166. Early Iron Maiden singer Dennis Wilcock quit the band when they refused to wear makeup like KISS.

167. Eddie and Alex Van Halen's original band "Mammoth" had no P.A. system of their own, so they'd rent David Lee Roth's system for $50 a night. After years of Eddie singing lead vocals, they figured they could save money by letting David Lee Roth into the band because he had the P.A. system.

168. Eddie Van Halen didn't ask for royalties or payment for completing Michael Jackson's "Beat it" guitar solo, he did it as a favor.

169. Eddie Van Halen donated 75 of his personal guitars to underfunded music education programs in public schools in Los Angeles.

170. Eddie Van Halen has designed his own line of guitars. First the Music Man "EVH", then the Peavey "Wolfgang", and now his own company called EVH partnering with Fender Musical Instruments. Eddie has always designed or modified his guitars, starting with the famous red and white striped Kramers.

171. Eddie Van Halen once auditioned for KISS.

172. On his 21st birthday in 1967, Keith Moon of The Who drove a Rolls Royce into the swimming pool of a Michigan hotel room.

173. Eddie Van Halen starting out playing drums. He bought a drum set and his brother bought a guitar. When his brother got better at drums than him, Eddie said "Ok. I'll play your guitar".

174. ELO's first album "The Electric Light Orchestra" has a different name in the U.S. The American record company tried to call and confirm the name of the album. When they failed to reach anyone on the phone, they wrote down "No Answer", which someone misconstrued as the name of the album.

175. Elton John's real name is Reginald Kenneth Dwight.

176. William Boyd and David Bowie created a fictional (hoax) artist called Nat Tate with an aim to expose the pretensions of the art world.

177. Elvis Presley borrowed elements of the black musicians he admired and went onto global domination.

178. Elvis Presley did not write any of the songs he sang.

179. Elvis Presley is known as "The King of Rock and Roll".

180. Elvis Presley is the best-selling solo artist of all time. Over one billion Elvis albums have been sold worldwide.

181. Elvis Presley made only one television commercial in his life, an ad for Southern Maid Doughnuts recorded on November 6, 1954.

182. Elvis Presley offered the press a chance to interview him in June of 1972 for a fee of $120,000. There were no takers.

183. Elvis Presley once asked his limo driver, "Do you own this limo, or do you work for the company?" He responded, "I

work for the company." Elvis said, "Well, you own it now." The limo driver's tip was the limo.

184. Elvis Presley once bought a random stranger a car after he saw her admiring his custom limo while it was parked at a car dealership.

185. Elvis Presley only ever failed in one class and it was music.

186. Elvis Presley recorded two songs for his mother's birthday in 1953 at Sun Records in Memphis, Tennessee. The songs were "My Happiness" and "That's When Your Heartache Begins".

187. Elvis Presley was a natural blonde but dyed his hair black so it would look better on the movie screen. He was inspired when he saw James Dean on film. He used Miss Clairol 51 D.

188. Elvis Presley was known for being so generous that he had problems not buying strangers and friends expensive gifts. Elvis's maid and cook Mary Jenkins was gifted six cars including three Cadillacs from him before his death. Elvis also gave his dentist and jeweler cars.

189. Elvis Presley was obsessed with Karate and even used his skills to fight off 4 attackers who came at him during a show.

190. Elvis Presley was so famous the Secret Service let him bring a Colt .45 into the White House to give to President Nixon.

191. Elvis Presley wore a cross, a star of David and the Hebrew letter chai. He said: "I don't want to miss out on heaven due to a technicality."

192. Rob Halford of Judas Priest broke his nose onstage and was rendered unconscious in 1990, during what was supposed to be his final show with the band. On the last show of the "Painkiller" tour in 1990, Halford was knocked off the motorcycle he famously rides onto the stage at the end of each show by a misplaced prop. He missed the last song of what was supposed to be his final show with Judas Priest.

193. Elvis Presley's favorite collectibles were official badges. He collected police badges in almost every city he performed in. He was also an avid gun collector. His collection of 40 weapons included M-16s and a Thompson submachine gun.

194. Parents of Metallica's James Hetfield were Christian Scientists and did not believe in medicine, so his mother died of cancer with no medical help.

195. Elvis Presley's manager (Colonel Tom Parker) sold "I Hate Elvis" badges to make money from those who otherwise would not have parted with their cash for Elvis merchandise.

196. Elvis Presley's name recognition worldwide is second, only to Jesus Christ.

197. The Trans-Siberian Orchestra has donated over $10,000,000 to charity since they started touring.

198. Following the deadly 1977 crash of the plane carrying the band Lynyrd Skynyrd into a Mississippi swamp, the survivors sought help at a nearby farmhouse, only to have the farmer who lived there shoot the band's drummer in the shoulder.

199. Elvis Presley's 1956 hit "Love Me Tender" was based on a sentimental Civil War ballad called "Aura Lee", first published in 1861.

200. "Stayin' Alive" by Bee Gees was used in a study to train medical staff to perform CPR. The song has close to 104 beats per minute, and 100-120 chest compressions per minute are recommended by the British Heart Foundation.

201. ZZ Top refused a $1,000,000 offer from Gillette to shave their beards for an ad.

202. Elvis Presley's father, Vernon Presley, died on June 26th, 1979, exactly two years after Elvis gave his final performance.

203. Elvis Presley's favorite movie was "Monty Python and The Holy Grail". He would sometimes rent out a movie theater to do midnight screenings of this movie with his friends.

204. Elvis Presley's October 1976 recording of "Way Down" also featured J.D. Sumner singing the words "way on down" at the end of each chorus, down to the note low C. At the end of the song he got down to double low C, which according to the Guinness Book Of World Records was the lowest note ever produced by the human voice up to that time.

205. Elvis recorded more than 600 songs but wrote none of them.

206. Elvis' mother, Gladys purchased his first guitar for him when he was 11 years old. He wanted a rifle, but his mother convinced him to get a guitar instead. It was purchased at Tupelo Hardware in Tupelo, Mississippi.

207. Eric Clapton wrote the song "Layla" with the intention of stealing George Harrison's wife.

208. Even though he has recorded some of the most memorable Rock 'n' Roll classics, the only Gold record that Chuck Berry ever received was for the 1972 novelty song, "My Ding-a-ling".

209. Every AC/DC album has gone to platinum status in the United States.

210. Exactly 700 actual beds were precisely laid out on a beach and used for the cover of Pink Floyd's album, "A Momentary Lapse of Reason". None of them were cardboard cutouts.

211. Exodus had to abandon early songs like "Impaler" and "Die by His Hand" because exiting guitarist Kirk Hammett repurposed parts of each song for Metallica's "Trapped Under Ice" and "Creeping Death".

212. Fidel Castro banned The Beatles and other bands in Cuba in 1964. He changed his mind two years later.

213. Finland has more heavy metal bands per capita than any other country in the world.

214. Flotsam and Jetsam got their name from a chapter title in J.R.R. Tolkien's "The Hobbit".

215. Following the death of Elvis, his record label made millions with Orion, a masked performer who sounded exactly like The King, leading many to believe he never really died.

216. Foo Fighters' Dave Grohl has his hero John Bonham's Led Zeppelin symbol tattooed on his arm.

217. For the album cover for "Breakfast Can Wait," Prince used the photo of Dave Chappelle dressed as Prince and serving pancakes, which was from a 2004 sketch from an episode of Chappelle's Show.

218. Frank Sinatra's acceptance speech for a Legend Award at the 1994 Grammys was cut short due to commercial breaks. In response, Billy Joel stopped halfway through his performance of 'The River of Dreams' later on, simply looking at his watch and saying 'valuable advertising time going by...'

219. Frank Zappa's Grammy-winning album "Jazz from Hell" received a "Parental Advisory" sticker even though it is a collection of instrumental pieces and contains no lyrics at all.

220. Freddie Mercury had a throat infection at the time of Live Aid concert and was advised by his doctors to not risk performing at the festival. He defied their orders, and Queen's set went down in history as one of the best performances that day.

221. An already inebriated Ace Frehley of KISS once drank an entire bottle of perfume after finding out it contained alcohol.

222. Metallica's first official song "Hit the Lights" was a carryover from James Hetfield's first band, Leather Charm.

223. Freddie Mercury is celebrated in Iran, a country where homosexuality is illegal, and Queen's "Bohemian Rhapsody" was the 1st rock song officially approved post-revolution since he calls for God in Arabic ("Bismillah! We will not let you go") to help regain his soul from Shaitan.

224. Freddie Mercury of Queen intended to record multiple duets with Michael Jackson, but after recording one song he dropped out of any further collaborations because he felt uncomfortable working with Jackson's pet llama in the studio.

225. Freddie Mercury spent his last month's recording as many vocals as he could for the rest of Queen to finish after his death.

226. Freddy Mercury was so ill with AIDS when he recorded "The Show Must Go On" that Brian May did not think he could do it. Mercury slammed some vodka, said "I'll fu*king do it, darling" and killed it in one take.

227. Future Motorhead singer Ian "Lemmy" Kilmister worked as a roadie for Jimi Hendrix.

228. Gene Simmons of KISS is reputed to have a tongue that is seven inches long, two inches longer than most men.

229. George Harrison's sister was married to an American, and the couple lived for a time in Herrin, Illinois, a small town in a coal-mining region of the Midwest. Harrison visited them in the United States before the Beatles were famous and even played the guitar on stage with some local bands.

230. George Young, who co-founded AC/DC along with his brothers Angus and Malcolm, was the lead guitarist for a band called The Easybeats, who scored a Billboard Top 20 hit in 1967 with "Friday On My Mind".

231. Glen Campbell played lead guitar on the recordings of The Beach Boys "Dance, Dance, Dance" and "Help Me Rhonda". He was also a full time member of The Beach Boys' touring group for four months in 1964 into 1965.

232. Glen Frey of The Eagles played rhythm guitar and sang backup vocals on Bob Seger's first Billboard Top 40 hit, "Ramblin', Gamblin' Man". The song reached #17 in 1969.

233. Green Day started a mud fight at Woodstock 1994. Amid the chaos, bouncers mistook bassist Mike Dirnt for a stage-invading fan and manhandled him so violently they knocked out some of his teeth.

234. Growing up in Indiana, Axl Rose attended church eight times a week, sang in the choir, and taught Sunday school.

235. Guitarist George Lynch shot his solo for Dokken's "You Just Got Lucky" video on a real, active volcano. It erupted only minutes after the final cut as the musician and crew escaped.

236. Guitarist James Murphy has no recollection of recording Testament's 1999 album "The Gathering" because his memories disappeared when he was operated on for a brain tumor soon after.

237. Guitarist Onnie McIntyre and drummer Robbie McIntosh, who later that year went on to form the Average White Band, played on Chuck Berry's 1972 hit, "My Ding-a-Ling".

238. Guitarist Peter Frampton was friend with David Bowie in school. His dad was head of the art department. He is gone on to play guitar with Bowie many times during his career.

239. Guitarist Terry Kath of the band Chicago died after he was cleaning his pistol and playing with it. His friend told him not to. Kath replied "It's not even loaded. What do you think I'm going to do, kill myself?" He then put the gun to his head and pulled the trigger. He was killed instantly.

240. Guitarist Steve Vai's hobby is beekeeping.

241. Guns N' Roses hit song Sweet Child o' Mine came under controversy in 2015 when a remarkably similar sounding track by a lesser known Australian rock band was discovered to have been released 6 years prior. Upon hearing the song, Guns N' Roses' bassist, Duff McKagan, called the similarities "stunning."

242. Bowie was the first sexually ambiguous British pop star, declaring himself bisexual in 1972 (before contemporaries such as Freddie Mercury and Elton John made similar declarations) and only five years since male homosexuality had been decriminalized in the UK. In a magazine interview, he stated that he met his first wife when they were in a relationship with the same man.

243. An unknown Freddie Mercury, at that time a London shoe stall assistant, fitted David Bowie for a pair of boots, over 10 years before "Under Pressure" was recorded.

Rock and Roll Facts

244. Elvis Presley's haircut was based on Captain Marvel Jr., commonly known as Freddy Freeman.

245. In the video for the song "One" Metallica used scenes taken from the anti-war film Johnny Got His Gun. And because their video was played a lot, Metallica were routinely required to pay royalty fees to continue showing the music video. So, Metallica bought the rights to the film.

246. Gwar's Oderus Urungus became the spokesman for Circuit City's video game commercials in the late 90s.

247. At a 1973 concert in California, The Who drummer Keith Moon passed out on stage after consuming horse tranquilizers and brandy. Unable to revive him, the band invited 19 year-old Scott Halpin on stage to finish the show.

248. Hoyt Axton wrote Three Dog Night's 1971 hit, "Joy to The World". His mother, Mae Axton co-wrote "Heartbreak Hotel" for Elvis Presley. Both songs topped the Billboard chart, making them the only Mother/Son duo to accomplish that feat.

249. In 1978, 30-year-old Ted Nugent became involved with 17-year-old Pele Massa. To get around the fact that she was under 18, Nugent convinced her parents to sign documents making him her legal guardian. They were then able to live

together freely and the pair remained intimate for almost a decade.

250. During a recording session, Black Sabbath guitarist Tony Iommi asked drummer Bill Ward if he could set him on fire. Ward replied, "not now but maybe later". A little time later Ward asked Tony if he still wanted to set him on fire. Tony replied he did. Iommi proceeded to pour gasoline on Ward resulting in third degree burns on his legs. Ward's mother later yelled at Iommi for setting her son on fire.

251. In 1938, Elvis Presley's father, Vernon, served nine months in the Parchman Penitentiary for altering a check. Elvis was just three years old at the time.

252. Van Halen frontman David Lee Roth allegedly paid his roadies extra money for finding the hottest groupies while on the road. Roth reportedly gave any roadie who picked the women he ultimately deemed worthy of bedding after a show an extra $100.

253. Metallica are the only U.S. band to have six consecutive studio albums debut at number one on the Billboard 200.

254. In 1947, a local radio show offered a young 12 year-old Elvis Presley a chance to sing live on-air, but he was too shy to go on.

255. In 1979, while Steve Vai was enrolled at the Berklee College of Music, he worked as a music transcriber for Frank Zappa.

256. In 1953, Bill Haley and His Comets are the first to hit the pop charts with a rock and roll song, "Crazy Man Crazy" which debuted at #12.

257. In 1954, Elvis auditioned for a gospel quartet named The Songfellows. They said he was not good enough.

258. In 1955, Sun Records founder Sam Phillips opened America's first all-female radio station, WHER in Memphis. When the station presented the foreign news, the ladies would amuse their listeners by announcing, "And now, the news from abroad."

259. In 1955, Billboard magazine published its annual disc jockey poll that named Elvis Presley as "the most promising Country and Western artist."

260. In 1956 Bette Nesmith Graham, the mother of Monkees guitarist Michael Nesmith, invented a correction fluid she called Mistake Out and founded the company that would become Liquid Paper. In 1979 the Liquid Paper Corporation was sold to the Gillette Corporation for $47.5 million.

261. In 1957, Elvis Presley asked his audience at a Seattle concert to please rise for the national anthem. He picked up his guitar, leaned in, shook his hips, and began his biggest hit "Hound Dog". A 15-year-old Jimi Hendrix was there.

262. In 1963 at the age of 11, Kurt Russell starred in a movie with Elvis Presley. 16 years later, a 27-year-old Russell played Elvis in a TV movie, and 15 years after that, voiced Elvis in Forrest Gump.

263. In 1963, The Rolling Stones' long hair style was considered controversial and outrageous. During this period, the members took out a Christmas ad in a newspaper stating, "Best wishes to all the starving hairdressers and their families."

264. In 1965, Ted Nugent heard of a Detroit group who had just broken up called "Amboy Dukes" and started using the name for his new band. "The Amboy Dukes" was the name of a novel about gang members and their lifestyle. In later interviews, Nugent said that although many people have given him a copy of the book, he has never actually read it.

265. In 1966, Brian Wilson of The Beach Boys spent six months recording, editing, and re-mixing "Good Vibrations" in seventeen different sessions, in four Los Angeles studios, at a cost of over sixteen thousand dollars. The recording engineer would later say that the last take sounded exactly like the first, six months earlier.

266. In 1967, The Beatles bought the Greek island of Leslo, surrounded by four smaller islands (one for each member of the band) but sold them a few months later as they were bored with the idea.

267. In 1969 Tommy James turned down an offer to perform at The Woodstock Festival after his booking agent described the event as "A stupid gig on a pig farm in Upstate New York." That decision cost the band millions in royalties.

268. In 1970, MGM records, under the leadership of President and future lieutenant governor of California, Mike Curb, canceled the recording contracts of 18 of their acts because they believed the performers promoted hard drugs in their songs. Among those who were dropped were squeaky clean night club performers Steve Lawrence and Eydie Gorme. Interestingly, they kept Eric Burdon and War, who made drug references in most of their songs.

269. During one of their live stage shows, ZZ Top decided to have a mixture of live animals, including vultures, buffaloes, and rattlesnakes on stage, but the buffalo rammed into a tank full of rattlesnakes and released them live on stage.

270. David Bowie was the First major artist to release a downloadable single in 1996.

271. Dark Horse Brewery turned down Nickelback endorsement deal because the workers hated the band.

272. Singer Tom Waits has a song called "The Fall of Troy", and Post-hardcore band "The Fall of Troy" has a song called "Tom Waits."

273. While recording his album "Antichrist Superstar", Marilyn Manson and his band found old bones poking out of the ground in a cemetery and proceeded to ground them up and smoke them.

274. In 1971 Pink Floyd played a show in London that was so loud it killed all the fish in a lake 100 yards away.

275. In 1972, Led Zeppelin was forced to cancel a concert in Singapore when officials would not let them off the plane because of their long hair.

276. In 1972, Leslie Harvey of Stone the Crows died after being electrocuted onstage in England. In 1976 Keith Relf, who used to play for The Yardbirds, was electrocuted by his guitar while playing in his basement.

277. In 2013, Kid Rock took a pay cut that cost him around $50,000 to $100,000 per night during his tour to keep ticket prices at $20 and a 12 ounce beer at $4.

278. A Megadeath is a unit of measurement. 1 Megadeath equal 1 million deaths caused by nuclear explosion. It is also where the band got its namesake.

279. In 1974, a then-unknown Queen performed at an Australian festival to a mean-spirited, drunken crowd. Before finishing, Freddie Mercury told them that Queen would be "one of the biggest bands in the world" the next time they visited. When they came back, they were at the top of the charts.

280. Black Crowes singer Chris Robinson was arrested in 1991 for an incident inside a 7-11 in Denver, Colo. Robinson was angry about not being able to buy booze after midnight. The woman made a comment that she'd "never heard of The Black Crowes" and Robinson promptly spit on her.

281. Ozzy Osbourne did not actually urinate on the Alamo. He urinated on the Alamo Cenotaph, a 60' high statue honoring the 189 Texans who died there during the Texas Revolution in 1836. The Cenotaph is located across the street from the Alamo.

282. In 1989, high on drugs, Slash punched through a glass door at an Arizona golf course, completely naked and in fear for his life, and grabbed a hotel maid to use as a "human shield" against the alien from the movie "Predator" that he thought was chasing him.

283. Metallica played a significant part in making Napster become a paid service in 2000.

284. In 1977, Aerosmith's flight crew inspected a Convair CV-240 for possible use as a tour plane and rejected it because they felt the plane and crew were not up to their standards. That plane crashed on October 20th, 1977 from fuel exhaustion due to poor maintenance, killing three members of Lynyrd Skynyrd.

285. In 1977, Emerson Lake and Palmer had 63 roadies, including a karate instructor for drummer Carl Palmer and the band's own doctor. It is rumored they also had a 'carpet roadie', whose job was to transport and sweep the Persian rug that Greg Lake stood on during the shows. A 70-piece orchestra joined that lot.

286. In 1977, three men were arrested for attempting to steal Elvis Presley's remains for ransom. This is why his body along with his mother's, was moved to Graceland where they are monitored by security.

287. In 1978, Aerosmith put up the money to bail out every fan arrested at one of their concerts for smoking marijuana.

288. In 1979 Italian punk band Skiantos brought a kitchen, a table, a TV, and a fridge onstage at a music festival, boiled some spaghetti and then ate it, without playing anything.

289. In 1979, tens of thousands of rock fans gathered at a Chicago stadium to destroy disco vinyl. That day became known as "the day disco died".

290. In 1984, Def Leppard's drummer Rick Allen had his left arm amputated after being in a serious car crash. It took him about two years of physical therapy, but he was able to continue as the band's drummer.

291. In 1984, Ozzy Osbourne and Mötley Crüe bassist, Nikki Sixx, had a competition to see who could outdo the other. Nikki licked some ants from a popsicle stick. Ozzy snorted a line of ants off the ground.

292. In 1984, Steven Tyler heard an old Aerosmith song on the radio and did not recognize it due to memory loss from years of drug use. He suggested to the band that they record a cover version. Joe Perry told him "It's us, fu*khead."

293. In 1986 the Red Hot Chili Peppers were budgeted $5000 by EMI Music to make a demo tape and set aside $2,000 to spend on heroin and cocaine.

294. In 1989, the U.S. military blared AC/DC music at General Noriega's compound in Panama for 2 continuous days. He surrendered.

295. In 1990, Chuck Berry was sued by several women who claimed that he had installed a video camera in the bathroom. Berry claimed that he had the camera installed to catch a worker who was suspected of stealing from the restaurant. Though his guilt was never proved in court, Berry opted for a class action settlement. One of his biographers, Bruce Pegg, estimated that, with 59 women, it cost Berry over $1.2 million plus legal fees.

296. In 1991, during a period of only six weeks, five classic modern rock albums were released: Metallica's Black Album, Pearl Jam's Ten, Guns 'N Roses' Use Your Illusion, Nirvana's Nevermind and Red Hot Chili Peppers' Blood Sugar Sex Magic. The last two were released on the same day.

297. In 1991, during a period of only six weeks, five classic modern rock albums were released: Metallica's Black Album, Pearl Jam's Ten, Guns N' Roses' Use Your Illusion, Nirvana's Nevermind and Red Hot Chili Peppers' Blood Sugar Sex Magic. The last two were released on the same day.

298. The Sex Pistol's "God Save the Queen", released during her silver jubilee, was considered controversial by the BBC and its spot on the top hits charts was left as an empty space.

299. In 1994, Guns N' Roses Bassist Duff McKagan bought $100,000 in stock in Microsoft, Amazon, and Starbucks.

300. In 1996, a small town in Utah mistakenly booked Rage Against the Machine at a venue for tractor and monster truck shows. The locals panicked and businesses boarded up thinking the band's followers would riot and vandalize everything.

301. In 1996, Ringo Starr appeared in a Japanese advertisement for apple sauce, which is what "Ringo" means in Japanese.

302. In 1996, Ringo Starr appeared in a Japanese advertisement for apple sauce. Coincidentally, "Ringo" means apple in Japanese.

303. In 1996, Rolling Stone Magazine readers named Weezer's "Pinkerton" the second worst album of the year.

304. In 2000, Yes keyboard player Rick Wakeman told BBC Radio 5 Live that he was hired to play piano on Cat Stevens' "Morning Has Broken" for 10 Pounds and was "shattered" that he was omitted from the credits, adding that he never received the money either. On his return to performing as Yusuf Islam, Stevens paid Wakeman and apologized for the original non-payment, which he said arose from confusion and a misunderstanding on the record label's part.

305. In 2006, the Rolling Stones staged a free concert at Copacabana Beach in Rio de Janeiro, Brazil. They played for two hours for a crowd of 1.5 million. Jagger addressed the crowd in Portuguese throughout the show.

306. In 2008 and at the age of 45, Flea, bass player of the multiplatinum rock band Red Hot Chili Peppers, enrolled as a freshman at University of Southern California's music program to learn the academic side of music.

307. In 2008, Prince covered Radiohead's "Creep" at Coachella. Someone uploaded a mobile video of it to YouTube. Prince quickly made YouTube remove it. After finding out about the blocking, Radiohead's lead singer Thom Yorke said "Well, tell him to unblock it. It's our song."

308. In 2009, Lamb of God frontman Randy Blythe played the part of a church deacon with anger issues in the movie "Graves".

309. In 2013, Metallica performed in Antarctica just to break a record and be the first musical act to perform on all 7 continents.

310. In 2014 it was reported that "Rock and Roll Part 2", co-written by Gary Glitter and Mike Leander, was earning an estimated $250,000 a year in royalties due to its use in the National Hockey League.

311. In 2014, Metallica's lead guitarist Kirk Hammett lost his phone that had over 250 ideas for riffs on it and did not have a backup. Because of this, he has no songwriting credits on subsequent album.

312. In April 1956, Elvis Presley tops the Pop Charts with his first RCA single release "Heartbreak Hotel". By the end of the year he would be the first artist to ever have nine singles in the Hot 100 at one time.

313. In August 2010, a religious group from Tempe, Arizona, put on a play named "Lamb of God", then they wondered why so many confused-looking heavy metal fans turned up for the first show.

314. In Australia, AC/DC are called Acca Dacca.

315. In early August 1966, about two weeks after Datebook magazine published John Lennon's infamous "We're more

popular than Jesus now" statement, The Beatles played at Dodger Stadium and were trapped inside the building by overzealous fans four about two hours. The two security guards assigned to protect them that day were named Jack Moses and Jim Christ.

316. In January 1978, guitarist Ted Nugent autographed a man's arm with a Bowie knife after the fan had requested it.

317. In May 1991, Freddie Mercury started recording vocals for "Mother Love", but upon reaching the last verse, he told his band that he had to "have a rest" and that he would return to finish it. He didn't end up making it to the studio, eventually succumbing to AIDS. Brian May sang the final verse.

318. In Melbourne, Australia, there is a street named AC/DC lane after the band.

319. In October 1979, The Guinness Book of World Records named Paul McCartney as the most successful composer of all time for writing 43 songs that sold over a million copies.

320. In terms of name recognition, Elvis Presley is second only to Jesus Christ worldwide.

321. In the 70's, Chuck Berry toured with only a guitar, finding some local bands for each show "confident that he could hire a band that already knew his music" and not even giving them a set list "and just expected the musicians to follow his lead".

322. In the song "Dirty deeds done dirt cheap" a phone number 36 – 24 – 36 is mentioned. This number belonged to a couple who later filed a lawsuit against the band as they claimed that they were being harassed by phone call from random people. The couple won the lawsuit and AC/DC had to shell out $250,000.

323. In the spring of 1983, Van Halen headlined the US Festival in San Bernardino, CA. They performed on "Heavy Metal Day" for the stratospheric fee of $1.5 million. The Guinness Book of World Records created an all-new category just for them: the highest paid single appearance of a band.

324. In the summer of 1967, Jimi Hendrix played seven gigs as the opening act for The Monkees

325. Iron Maiden's "Can I Play with Madness" video included a cameo from Monty Python icon Graham Chapman, who played an ornery professor. He died just over a year later.

326. It was at a concert in Minneapolis in 1954 that Al Dvorin first closed Elvis's concerts with: "Ladies and Gentlemen, Elvis has left the building. Thank you and good night."

327. It was Paul McCartney, not Ringo Starr who played drums on The Beatles' "The Ballad of John and Yoko".

328. Jan Berry of Jan And Dean was reported to have an I.Q. of 180, which puts him well into the genius category.

329. Jeremy Spencer left the band Fleetwood Mac to join a cult known as Children of God.

330. "Crazy Little Thing Called Love" was written by Freddie Mercury in 10 minutes as a tribute to Elvis Presley.

331. Jerry Lee Lewis married his 13 year-old cousin.

332. Jimi Hendrix and his girlfriend Kathy Etchingham called each other by their middle names, Marshall, and Mary. After an argument where Jimi complained about her lumpy mashed potatoes, Etchingham stormed out into the street and left. When she returned the next day, he had written 'The Wind Cries Mary.'

333. Jimi Hendrix created the song "Little Wing" in 145 seconds.

334. Jimi Hendrix died on September 18th, 1970. The post-mortem revealed that he had vomited in his sleep and choked to death having overdosed on sleeping tablets.

335. Jimi Hendrix dropped out of high school and enlisted in the Army in May 1959. He was a member of the "Screaming Eagles" 101st Airborne Division in Fort Campbell, Kentucky as a trainee paratrooper.

336. Jimi Hendrix originally toured the United States as the opening act for The Monkees.

337. Jimi Hendrix was once invited to play with Cream alongside Eric Clapton. In the middle of the show, Clapton walked off stage. He was found in the back shaking angrily and smoking a cigarette. When asked what was wrong, he simply replied, "You never told me he was that f*cking good."

338. Jimi Hendrix was the highest paid performer at Woodstock. He was paid $18,000.

339. Jimi Hendrix's performance of 'The Star Spangled Banner" at Woodstock was a protest to America's involvement in the Vietnam war.

340. Joe Perry and Brad Whitford didn't play the solos on Aerosmith's classic rendition of "Train Kept a Rollin'". The intro solo was played by Steve Hunter and the second solo over the simulated live audience was performed by Dick Wagner. Neither guitarist got credit on the album for their parts.

341. Joe Satriani has been nominated for a Grammy 15 times.

342. Joe Satriani is the highest-selling instrumental guitarist of all time.

343. Joe Walsh and Ringo Starr are brothers-in-law. Starr is married to Barbara Bach, who is the sister of Walsh's wife, Marjorie.

344. John Bonham, the drummer for Led Zeppelin, drank 40 shots of vodka the night of his death.

345. John Fogerty of Creedence Clearwater Revival had never been to Mississippi when he wrote "Proud Mary" or Louisiana when he penned "Born on The Bayou".

346. Def Jam Records founder Rick Rubin was in a punk band called 'The Pricks' that asked friends to heckle during a gig in order to start a brawl leading to the band being kicked

off stage & the show being shut down by a "cop" who was really Rubin's father, in an effort to create buzz around the band.

347. Freddie Mercury died due to complications from AIDS just one day after announcing his condition publicly.

348. John Lennon admitted to physically abusing both of his wives, Cynthia and Yoko. In an interview with Playboy magazine he said, "I was a hitter. I couldn't express myself and I hit."

349. John Lennon was shot to death by Mark David Chapman outside of his apartment in New York on December 8th, 1980.

350. John Lennon wrote "Good Morning, Good Morning" after hearing a Corn Flakes commercial.

351. There is a spider named after David Bowie, the 'Heteropoda davidbowie.'

352. John Lennon's father was absent for much of his early life but showed up when Lennon became famous.

Rock and Roll Facts

353. Johnny Depp said he used Marilyn Manson as an inspiration for his role as Charlie in "Charlie and the Chocolate Factory".

354. David Bowie was briefly banned from SNL in 1997 for playing a song that reminded Lorne Michaels too much of the time when he was a heavy coke user.

355. Jon Bon Jovi has a community restaurant that has no prices listed for the food. You pay for it if you can afford to or volunteer in the kitchen in exchange for meals.

356. Jon Bon Jovi owns the band. The other members are his employees.

357. Jon Bon Jovi's real name is John Bongiovi.

358. Jónsi, the lead singer in Sigur Rós, once forgot the lyrics while performing with the band in France. He improvised and kept on singing in Icelandic "Oh sh*t, I forgot the lyrics, but that's o.k. because I'm in France where no one understands me."

359. Journey formed in 1973 in San Francisco, California. However, Steve Perry did not join the band until 1977.

360. Journey, formed in 1973 by guitarist Neal Schon, was originally called Golden Gate Rhythm Section. Journey has sold more than 70 million albums.

361. Juda Priest got their name from Bob Dylan's 1967 song, "The Ballad of Frankie Lee and Judas Priest".

362. Judas Priest singer Rob Halford briefly worked at a pornographic theater before joining the band.

363. Kansas was interviewed for an episode of VH-1's "Behind the Music" but the episode was never aired because the show's producers thought the band's lives were too dull and boring.

364. Keith Moon of The Who, named Led Zeppelin when he said that Zeppelin guitarist's new band will "go down like a lead balloon".

365. Keith Richards heard the riff to "(I Can't Get No) Satisfaction" in a dream. He woke up, played the riff on a tape recorder and mumbled "I can't get no satisfaction" and went back to sleep.

366. Keith Richards was arrested in 1977, for heroin possession. As part of his sentence, he played two shows in Toronto for blind children.

367. Kirk Hammett encouraged Les Claypool to audition for Metallica after Cliff Burton died. After not getting the job, James Hetfield said it was because Claypool was "too good" and "should do his own thing."

368. Kirriemuir, where Bon Scott was born, is in the county of Angus. Bon's mother Isa's maiden name was Mitchell, which is Malcolm Young's middle name.

369. Korn bassist Fieldy has a tattoo done by Limp Bizkit singer Fred Durst when Durst still worked in a Florida tattoo parlor.

370. Kurt Cobain did not know that Teen Spirit was a brand of deodorant when he wrote "Smells Like Teen Spirit." Cobain took the idea for the song's title from Bikini Kill's Kathleen Hanna, who had written "Kurt smells like Teen Spirit" on his apartment wall.

371. Led Zeppelin and Pink Floyd members helped to fund the making of Monty Python and the Holy Grail.

372. Led Zeppelin got their name from The Who drummer, Keith Moon, who said "your band will go down like a lead balloon".

373. Led Zeppelin guitarist and founder, Jimmy Page, dated a 14-year-old while on tour with the band.

374. Led Zeppelin let Ben Affleck use "When the Levee Breaks" in Argo with the condition that they digitally alter the player's needle drop to the correct spot on the record.

375. Led Zeppelin once rented six floors of the Andaz Hotel in West Hollywood, California for their entourage and friends, hosting a drug-fueled orgy while drummer John Bonham rode a motorcycle down hotel corridors.

376. Led Zeppelin was sued by the band Spirit for stealing the famous intro to "Stairway to Heaven" from its song "Taurus".

377. Led Zeppelin's first show together took place after just 15 hours of practicing together at the Gladsaxe Teen Club in Gladsaxe, Denmark, at 5:30 p.m. local time on Saturday, September 7, 1968. The set list included "You Shook Me," "Dazed and Confused," and "Train Kept-A-Rollin." At this gig they were called The New Yardbirds.

378. Legendary comedian Milton Berle agreed to appear in Ratt's "Round and Round" video because his nephew Marshall Berle, was Ratt's manager at the time.

379. Legendary director George Lucas was one of the cameramen on the band's 1970 documentary, "Gimme Shelter".

380. Legendary rock photographer Neil Zlozower got his start to his long and illustrious career at the age of 16 years old. He has gone on to shoot some of the most iconic photos of Mötley Crüe, Van Halen, Led Zeppelin, AC/DC, Frank Zappa, Ozzy Osbourne, Randy Rhoads among thousands of others.

381. Leo Fender, who founded the Fender Electric Instrument Manufacturing Company, whose products included the iconic Telecaster and Stratocaster guitars, never learned to play the instruments which he made a career of building.

382. Les Paul is the only person to be included in both the Rock and Roll Hall of Fame and the National Inventors Hall of Fame.

383. Linsey Buckingham and Stevie Nicks were recruited to join Fleetwood Mac after Mick Fleetwood visited the Sound City recording studio and asked to hear the most recent album recorded there.

384. Little Richard is a pioneer of rock and roll and helped define its sound in the early 50s.

385. Little Richard kicked Jimi Hendrix out of his band in the 50's. Apparently, Hendrix refused to wear the band uniform and would steal audience's attention with his eccentric style and guitar skills.

386. Little Richard's father, Charles "Bud" Penniman was both a church deacon and a nightclub owner who sold bootlegged moonshine on the side.

387. Lynyrd Skynyrd got its name from a high school P.E. teacher, Leonard Skinner.

388. Lynyrd Skynyrd's Ronnie Van Zant is said to be buried with a Neil Young t-shirt, the same he uses on his last cd cover. The admiration between these two musicians was mutual: Young said he would rather play "Sweet Home Alabama" than "Southern Man" (his own southern anthem).

389. Malcom Young used to play the solos in AC/DC, until one day he told his brother to do them because it interfered with his drinking.

390. Marilyn Manson did not play "Paul" on the TV show "The Wonder Years". That role was played by Josh Saviano.

391. Queen's collaboration with David Bowie on 'Under Pressure' was not planned. Bowie just happened to be by the studio while Queen were recording the song.

392. Marilyn Manson sometimes writes the word "F**K" across his face so paparazzi cannot sell photos of him.

393. Marshall Tucker acquired their name from a piano tuner whose named was found on a key ring in their old rehearsal space.

394. Marty Friedman of Megadeth is so fluent in Japanese that he once won a competition sponsored by Arizona State University to speak Japanese and write a paper on it in traditional Japanese. He then had to speak to a panel of Japanese judges in their language. He came in first place.

395. Maxim magazine ranked former Rolling Stones bassist Bill Wyman at number 10 on its Living Sex Legends list, as he is reputed to have had sex with over 1,000 women.

396. Metallica is the first and only band to play on all seven continents.

397. Metallica spent roughly $400,000 on the music video for The Memory remains.

398. Metallica was told that expletives were prohibited during their performance at the 1996 MTV Europe awards performance. They were expected to play a slow song from their new album. Instead, they played the two most offensive songs that they had.

399. Metallica wrote the song "The God That Failed" because Hetfield's mother died due to Christian beliefs influencing her decision to reject cancer treatment.

400. Metallica, Anthrax, Mötley Crüe, Napalm Death, Slayer and Sonic Youth all formed in 1981.

401. Metallica's Cliff Burton and Kirk Hammett drew cards to decide who would get to choose a bunk on their tour bus in 1986. Burton drew the Ace of Spades, chose the bunk Hammett had been occupying, and was thrown out of the window and crushed when the bus crashed. He died at the scene.

402. Metallica's lawyer once sent a cease and desist letter to a Metallica cover band. Metallica later said they had no idea the letter had been sent and offered an apology and told Rolling Stone that they had started out as a cover band, adding "Heck, we even recorded a two-disc album of covers!"

403. Michael Jackson bought the rights to most of The Beatles music for $47.5 million in 1985. It is now worth $450 million.

404. Michael Jackson paid $47 million for the publishing rights to the Beatles' back catalogue in 1985 and sold a share of it to Sony in 1995 for $95 million.

405. Mick Jagger is an experienced ballet dancer with years of lessons under his belt.

406. The woman on the cover of Black Sabbath's debut album is model Luisa Livingstone, who was cast in part because she was only 5' tall and would make everything else look bigger.

407. Mick Jagger once said that he thought The Rolling Stones would only last a couple of years. He said, "I'd rather be dead than sing "Satisfaction" when I'm 45."

408. Musician Jack Johnson donated 100% of his 2008 tour profits to charity. His tours since have donated to and supported many environmental charities local to where the band plays.

409. In 1998, musician David Bowie launched a dial-up Internet Service Provider known as "BowieNet", which

came with its own email and exclusive content. The service lasted till 2006.

410. Mick Mars of Mötley Crüe originally played in a band called Motley Croo in the early '70s.

411. More than 2,200 cover versions of The Beatles' "Yesterday" exist, making it one of the most recorded songs in history.

412. Morrisey was invited to appear on the TV show friends but declined because he did not want to sing with Phoebe.

413. Motorhead drummer Phil "Philthy Animal" Taylor has an orange-sized lump on the back of his neck, the result of breaking his neck on tour in the early 80s and forgetting to visit a doctor for years.

414. Motorhead's Lemmy got his nickname because he was always asking friends to borrow money, as in "lemmy some money".

415. Mudhoney bassist Guy Maddison considers his duties in the band secondary to his career as a registered nurse.

416. Napalm Death got into the Guinness Book of World Records with the shortest song ever: "You Suffer" which lasts just 1.316 seconds.

417. Neal Schon is the only original member of Journey that never left the band.

418. The first printing of the "Metal Massacre" album had Metallica's named spelled wrong with two "t's".

419. Neil Young and Rick James were in a band together in the early 60s called Myrnah Birds. The band was signed to Motown Records but broke up soon after when Rick James was arrested for going AWOL from the military.

420. Matt Barlow of Iced Earth was a policeman and after the 9/11 attacks he left the band to work as a policeman again. He returned to music in 2007.

421. Musician Billy Squier effectively derailed his career by releasing a video for the song 'Rock Me Tonite' that had him dancing around in a pink shirt.

422. Neil Young once wired up his house to be the left speaker and the barn as his right speaker so that he could listen to music from a boat in the middle of his lake.

423. Jimi Hendrix and James Brown were both backing musicians for Little Richard early in their careers. When Richard couldn't make some shows because of a scheduling conflict, James Brown would fill in by impersonating Richard.

424. After the death of musician Gram Parsons, his manager and assistant stole his body from an airport and an unsuspecting patrolman helped them load it into a hearse. They then took the body to Joshua Tree National Park, covered it with gasoline, and set it on fire.

425. Neil Young wrote "Cinnamon Girl", "Down by the River", the title track, and "Cowgirl in the Sand", all on a single day while suffering from a 103 degree Fahrenheit fever.

426. Nightwish's song "Nemo" is based on the Latin word for "Nobody". But many fans presume it references the Disney movie and have been known to toss clownfish plush toys at the band in concert.

427. Freddie Mercury bequeathed much of his fortune to his ex-girlfriend, Mary Austin, and entrusted her to ensure that the burial place of his ashes would never be disclosed.

428. The musician Gary Numan, who had the hit "Cars" in 1980, became an accomplished aerobatic display pilot and

performed at airshows. He finally hung it up after having kids.

429. The oldest musicians ever in to have a hit on the charts were the Zimmers in 2007 with their version of "My Generation". Lead singer Alf Carretta was 90, drummer Buster Martin was 100 and the combined age of their 40 members was 3120 years(average age of 78).

430. Nirvana and Soundgarden shared a member named Jason Everman who went on to become a Green Beret.

431. Nirvana purposely hired a bad video director, Sam Bayer, so that the music video for Smells Like Teen Spirit would turn out to be rough and 'not corporate' like. But the video was so well received that it gave the band, along with MTV, major corporate success.

432. Nirvana was adamantly told not to play the song "Rape Me" at the 1992 MTV Music Awards. Nevertheless, at the start of the performance, Cobain started playing the chords to "Rape Me" as MTV producers watched in horror. He then switched back to "Lithium", as scheduled.

433. None of Elvis Presley's movies ever got nominated for Oscar, but he did win three Grammy Awards, for his gospel recordings.

434. None of The Beatles could read music.

435. Not long before his death, Freddie Mercury, confined to his bed, got to see an advance copy of the "Wayne's World" scene with Wayne and Garth headbanging to "Bohemian Rhapsody". He loved it and approved of the song's use in the film. The movie, in part, helped launch Queen's comeback in the United States.

436. Of all the singers of the top 5 bands of the Grunge era, only Eddie Vedder from Pearl Jam is still alive. Kurt Cobain, Layne Staley, Chris Cornell, and Scott Weiland have all died.

437. Before he became Jon Bon Jovi, aspiring musician John Bongiovi made his recorded debut in a somewhat inauspicious manner, singing on a Star Wars-themed Christmas album. The song was called 'R2-D2, We Wish You a Merry Christmas.'

438. Of Bruce Springsteen's nineteen Billboard Top 40 hits, none have ever topped the list. His highest charting single was 1984's "Dancing in The Dark", which reached #2.

439. On February 3rd, 1959, three of the biggest rock and roll stars at the time all died in a plane crash together: Buddy Holly, The Big Bopper and Richie Valens. They died near Clear Lake, Iowa when their single-engine Beechcraft Bonanza plane crashed into a field, killing them instantly.

440. On his last day as a welder, Tony Iommi, guitarist of Black Sabbath, lost the tips of his two fretting fingers. While he was recovering, he found it easier to play the guitar by dropping the tuning and using lighter gauge strings, which helped give Black Sabbath its signature, dark, sound.

441. On September 19, 1985, when Frank Zappa famously testified before Congress to protest the PMRC's attempt to legislate and censor heavy metal music lyrics, Zappa compared the proposed legislation to "treating dandruff by decapitation".

442. On the cover of Iron Maiden's "Powerslave" album, artist Derek Riggs inserted secret messages into the detailed Egyptian artwork including Mickey Mouse and phrases like "bollocks" and "Indiana Jones was here".

443. On the death of his mother, Jimi Hendrix's father refused to take him to the funeral, instead giving the then 15-year-old shots of whiskey and informing him that this was how men dealt with loss.

444. On the Red Hot Chili Peppers' album "One Hot Minute", "Tearjerker" is about Kurt Cobain and "Transcending" is about River Phoenix.

445. One night at a gig, when The Who had just begun, Pete Townshend was experimenting with the feedback he got

when he put his guitar near his amp. He accidentally hit the ceiling with the guitar, which caused an awesome sound that was cheered by the small audience. Townshend tried to repeat that sound with such bad luck that he broke the guitar's neck. "No one cheered, in fact there was a terrible silence, so I finished breaking the guitar acting as if that had been my true intention". On The Who's next performance there were twice as many people.

446. David Bowie recorded "China Girl" to pull Iggy Pop from financial ruin.

447. One of the highest-attended concerts in history was held by Metallica on September 28, 1991 at Tushino Airfield in Moscow where 1.6 million people attended.

448. One of the tunes that Brian Wilson recorded for his "Live at the Roxy Theatre" album in 2000 is the Barenaked Ladies' 1992 song "Brian Wilson", which poked fun at the time that he spent in bed in the 1970s.

449. One time Kurt Cobain and Pat Smear heard Dave Grohl playing the guitar backstage, and one said to the other "We're not even the best guitar players in Nirvana."

450. Original Iron Maiden vocalist Paul Di'anno hired instrumental rock band LoNero to be his backing band on his U.S. tour of 50 dates. Unfortunately, all shows were

canceled after Di'anno was denied his passport to the United States due to disability fraud.

451. Ozzy Osbourne guitarist Randy Rhoads died in a plane crash on March 19th, 1982 in Leesburg, Florida. The pilot buzzed the tour bus that Ozzy was on with the rest of the band and the wing clipped the bus, killing Randy, the pilot and seamstress Rachel Youngblood, instantly.

452. Paramore broke "The Nashville Curse" by being the first band from the Tennessee city to have an album go platinum in 20 years.

453. Paul McCartney admitted the "you" in the song "Got to Get You into My Life" was marijuana.

454. Paul McCartney and John Lennon wrote "I Wanna Be Your Man" for The Rolling Stones.

455. There was a note in the booklet of Freddie Mercury's album "Mr. Bad Guy" which read: "This album is dedicated to my cat Jerry. Also, Tom, Oscar and Tiffany, and all the cat lovers across the universe. Screw everybody else!"

456. Steve Vai followed a strict practice routine of playing his guitar for 10 to 15 hours a day in a structured and rigid manner.

457. Paul McCartney performed in the opening ceremony of the 2012 London Olympics for a mere $1.57.

458. Paul McCartney was the last bachelor Beetle when he married Linda Eastman in a civil ceremony in London, 1969. Paul's brother Mike was his best man. No other Beetle attended the wedding.

459. Paul McCartney wrote The Beatles song "Yesterday" in his sleep. When he woke up, he went to the piano to play the chords. He then played it for everyone he could for months to make sure it was not a song that had already been recorded.

460. Paul McCartney's younger brother, Michael, formed a comedy/music group of his own in 1962 called The Scaffold. In 1968 they topped the U.K. chart with a song called "Lily the Pink". Known professionally as Mike McGear, he is mentioned in the lyric of "Let 'Em In" as Brother Michael.

461. Pearl Jam originally named themselves "Mookie Blaylock" after the New Jersey Nets basketball player and named their debut album "Ten" after his Jersey number.

462. Pearl Jam were Neil Young's backing band on the album "Mirror Ball" but were not mentioned in the credits for contractual reasons.

463. Pearl Jam's cover of "Last Kiss" only cost them $1,000 to record, it is also their highest charting hit to date, peaking at No. 2 on the Billboard Hot 100.

464. Pete Townshend has smashed more than 90 guitars in his Who career, including at least 23 Fender Stratocasters, 12 Gibson Les Pauls and 21 Gibson SGs.

465. Pete Townshend thought he was lifting his now-famous Windmill move from Keith Richards, because Pete saw Keith doing it as the curtain was rising at a Stones show. Later, after Pete had made it his big move, he talked with Keith about it and realized Keith was just stretching out his arm before starting to play.

466. David Bowie refused Knighthood in 2003, which would have made him Sir David Bowie. He said, "I would never have any intention of accepting anything like that. I seriously do not know what it's for. It's not what I spent my life working for."

467. Peter Grant, Led Zeppelin's manager, is reported to have secured 90% of gate money from concerts performed by them. His trust and loyalty to Led Zeppelin was such that his managerial arrangement with the band was via a gentlemen's agreement.

468. Peter Green left Fleetwood Mac to become a farmer.

469. Phil Lynott of Thin Lizzy died on January 4th, 1986. The official cause of death was "multiple internal abscesses causing blood poisoning leading to kidney, liver and heart failure."

470. Pink Floyd performed under various monikers in their early years, including Tea Set, Sigma 6, The Screaming Abdabs and Leonard's Lodgers.

471. Pink Floyd's "Dark Side of the Moon" earnings were invested in a floating restaurant, a fudge-making hotel, a computer game, a film nobody saw, a skateboard company, a car hire business, and a children's shoe factory. All complete failures. They fled to France as tax exiles and recorded "The Wall".

472. Pink Floyd's "Dark Side of the Moon" album was so popular; it had a German factory pressing nothing but that album 34 years after it was first released.

473. Pink Floyd's "Dark Side of the Moon" spent 741 weeks on the billboard charts, from 1973 to 1988, longer than any other album.

474. Pink Floyd's album "The Wall" is cyclical, with the phrase "Isn't this where..." "...we came in?" split in half between the first and last song. When the two songs are spliced together, the complete phrase "Isn't this where we came in?" forms, proposing that Pink's story repeats itself.

475. Pink Floyd's original name was Sigma 6. The band included Roger Waters on bass, Nick Mason on drums, Richard Wright on keyboard, Bob Close on guitar, and Syd Barret also on guitar. With Syd's influence, the band changed their name to The Pink Floyd Sound, named after Pink Anderson and Floyd Council (two bluesmen).

476. Platinum selling guitarist, Joe Satriani was the guitar teacher for Steve Vai (Frank Zappa/David Lee Roth/Whitesnake), Kirk Hammet (Metallica), Larry LaLonde (Primus), Alex Skolnick (Testament) and Charlie Hunter.

477. Prince played 27 different instruments on his debut album "For You".

478. Prince used the heartbeat of his unborn son as part of the percussion in one track on the "Emancipation" album. By the time the album was released, his son had died of a congenital birth defect.

479. Musician Moby's real name is Richard. He calls himself 'Moby' after "Moby Dick", which was written by his great-great-great-great uncle Herman Melville.

480. Prince would play concerts as a "cover" in areas affected by natural disasters so that he could be in cities where he could offer help. Because of his faith as a Jehovah's Witness

he could not, and wouldn't, ever speak publicly about any of his charitable acts.

481. Elvis Presley's doctor prescribed him more than 10,000 doses of sedatives, amphetamines, and narcotics in just first eight months of 1977.

482. Prince's song "Purple Rain" is a tribute to Jimi Hendrix's "Purple Haze".

483. Prior to their music careers, Sid Vicious and Johnny Rotten of The Sex Pistols, would often perform Alice Cooper covers on the streets for money. People would pay them to stop.

484. Queen guitarist Brian May built his primary guitar, the "Red Special" when he was 16. It contains parts from a motorbike, bicycle, knitting needle, and the wood is from a 18th-century fireplace mantel.

485. Queen guitarist Brian May developed hepatitis from a tainted needle in 1974, almost forcing him to have his arm amputated. He eventually regained his health in time to help his bandmates finish the album which contained their first mega hit, "Killer Queen".

486. Queen holds the Guinness World Record for longest-running rock group fan club.

487. Queen is the only group that has had all of its members compose multiple #1 hits, so in addition to the band being inducted into the Rock and Roll Hall of Fame, all four members have been individually inducted into the Songwriters Hall of Fame.

488. Queen lead singer Freddie Mercury once dressed Princess Diana up in drag and took her to a gay bar.

489. Queen originally were not going to release the song "Another One Bites the Dust", but when Michael Jackson heard the song backstage at an L.A. concert, he convinced the band to release it.

490. Queen, Bob Marley never won a Grammy while Milli Vanilli and Justin Bieber did.

491. Queen's Brian May uses a sixpence British coin instead of a guitar pick and occasionally uses its serrated edge against the strings for certain sounds.'

492. Red Hot Chili Peppers recorded "Blood Sugar Sex Magik" in a haunted house once owned by Harry Houdini.

493. Richie Haven's most famous song "Freedom" was improvised on stage at Woodstock.

494. Robert Kennedy was assassinated during the exact same week that the Rolling Stones were recording 'Sympathy for the Devil.' The original lyrics were "I shouted out 'Who killed Kennedy?'" but Jagger changed it to "I shouted out 'Who killed the Kennedys?'"

495. Rock and Roll developed from an early version of Rhythm and Blues.

496. Rock music encompasses many genres including punk, hard rock, heavy metal, thrash, progressive, rockabilly, death metal, folk rock, pop rock, surf rock, southern rock, Latin rock, glam metal, blues rock, psychedelic rock, jazz rock and more.

497. Rock 'n' Roll Hall of Fame member Chuck Berry served three jail terms: two and half years for armed robbery in 1944, twenty months for violation of The Mann Act in 1959, and four months for tax evasion in 1979.

498. Rolling Stones drummer, Charlie Watts, was sleeping one day, when Mick Jagger phoned drunk to Watts' hotel room asking where his drummer was. Watts got up, suited-up, went to Jagger's room, punched him, and then replied: "Don't ever call me your drummer again. You're my f**king singer!"

499. Ronnie James Dio was recommended to Black Sabbath by former Sabbath vocalist Ozzy Osbourne's wife Sharon.

500. Roxie Roker, the neighbor on the TV show "The Jeffersons" was the mother of singer Lenny Kravitz.

501. Sammy Hagar owns his own restaurant chain called Cabo Wabo Cantina. He was also owner of Cabo Wabo Tequila but sold the company.

502. Scatman John suffered from a severe stutter from the time he learned to speak, which led to an emotionally traumatic childhood. He then made the song, "Scatman," in which he intended to inspire children who stuttered to overcome the condition. It reached #1 in 13 countries.

503. Scotty Moore, the original guitarist for Elvis Presley was home one day when he got a call from Keith Richards. Richards invited him to the Rolling Stones' show that night. Scotty told Richards that he could not go because he had some important things to take care of. When he hung up the phone, his friend asked him what he had to do, Scotty replied "work in my garden".

504. Sebastian Bach auditioned for Velvet Revolver in 2002 but Slash said it sounded too much like Skid Row.

505. Session drummer Hal Blaine played on every Record of The Year Grammy winner between 1966 and 1971, as well as 150 Top Ten singles and 40 Number Ones.

506. Several of the major forces in the world of Rock 'n' Roll, including Jimi Hendrix and The Carpenters, started out as opening acts for Engelbert Humperdinck in the late '60s, '70's and '80s.

507. Sharks act calmer when listening to AC/DC.

508. Sid Vicious is credited with inventing the Pogo move where you bounce up and down with the music.

509. Singer Bryan Adams, photographed Queen Elizabeth II for a Canadian postage stamp.

510. Slash from the band Guns N' Roses refused to allow "Glee" to use the band's music because he thought the show sucked.

511. Slash plays guitar on Michael Jackson's song "Black or White".

512. Slash's real name is Saul Hudson.

513. Social Distortion was formed in Fullerton, California by Mike Ness in 1979

514. Social Distortion's 1990 cover of "Ring of Fire" is the most commercially successful cover of the Johnny Cash classic, reaching No. 25 on the Billboard modern rock chart 27 years after the song was first recorded by the country music legend.

515. It was Freddie Mercury's dying wish for "Bohemian Rhapsody" to be reissued to raise money for AIDS charities. When the song was rereleased in late 1991, it topped the charts, staying at #1 for five weeks for the first time since its debut in 1975.

516. Punk rock band The Clash was named by guitarist Mick Jones, who chose the name because he noticed that the word "clash" appeared to come up frequently in newspaper headlines.

517. Some proponents of the "Elvis Is Alive" theory maintain that when a document examiner analyzed the handwriting on Elvis Presley's death certificate, he found that it matches the handwriting of Elvis himself.

518. Static-X lead singer Wayne Static was once in a band named Deep Blue Dream with Smashing Pumpkins singer Billy Corgan.

519. Steven Tyler and Joe Perry were once known as the Toxic Twins due to their abuse of drugs in the early days of Aerosmith.

520. KISS guitarist Vinnie Vincent once wrote music for "Happy Days and "Joanie Loved Chachi". He used to sit at the Cunningham's dining room table and write songs on an acoustic guitar.

521. Steven Tyler of Aerosmith wrote "Dude Looks Like a Lady" after seeing Vince Neil from Mötley Crüe.

522. Steven Tyler wrote "Dream On" when he was 16 years old.

523. Stevie Nicks was offered the opportunity to write the lyrics for "Purple Rain" by Prince but turned it down.

524. Stevie Nicks wrote Stand Back while listening to Prince's Little Red Corvette. Because Stevie wrote Stand Back using the exact music for Little Red Corvette, she called Prince to tell him about the song, and he showed up at her studio 25 minutes later to record the synthesizers for it.

525. Stevie Ray Vaughan was the guitarist on David Bowie's "Let's Dance" album.

526. Swedish band Meshuggah derived their name from the Yiddish word for "crazy".

527. System of a Down's name was inspired by a Daron Malakian poem called "Victims of a Down" but they decided on "System" partly because their albums could sit closer to Slayer's in record store bins.

528. Ten days before Freddie Mercury died, Jim Beach, Queen's manager, met with him to discuss what could be done with his legacy. Freddie quipped, "You can do whatever you like with my image, my music, remix it, re-release it, whatever... just never make me boring."

529. Termites will eat wood two times faster when listening to heavy metal.

530. Testament singer Chuck Billy and Deftones guitarist Stephen Carpenter are first cousins.

531. The American Rock Band 'The Postal Service' was sent a cease and desist letter by the United States Postal Service for trademark infringement of their name. After negotiations,

the USPS allowed the band to use their name in exchange for playing a free show at their national conference.

532. Contrary to belief, Marilyn Manson did not have a rib removed so he could suck his own penis.

533. The Animals first organized as a Jazz quintet with Eric Burdon on trombone. Partly because Burdon was not a good player, he took up singing and the band switched to Rock 'n' Roll.

534. Van Morrison was tied into a horrible record contract that wanted 36 songs out of him before he could get out of the deal. So, he recorded 30 songs in one day.

535. Sid Vicious of The Sex Pistols once shot up toilet water filled with urine and vomit.

536. The band Creed once put on such a bad show that a $2,000,000 class action lawsuit was filed on behalf of all the fans in attendance.

537. The band Ghost inspired "The Ghost" burger served in a Chicago restaurant. Its recipe includes goat shoulder, red wine reduction and a communion wafer.

538. The Band recorded their second studio album in the pool house of a home once owned by Judy Garland, Wally Cox and, at the time the group worked there, Sammy Davis, Jr.

539. The Beach Boys had two Billboard Top Ten hits in 1964 that consisted of just one word repeated three times: "Fun, Fun, Fun" (#5) and "Dance, Dance, Dance" (#8).

540. The Beach Boys once recorded a song by Charles Manson. The song was originally titled "Cease to Exist" but was renamed "Never Learn Not to Love".

541. The Beach Boys' classic 1966 album 'Pet Sounds' is named after something Mike Love said when Brian Wilson showed him the new material. "Who the hell is going to listen to this?" he reportedly asked, "the ears of a dog?"

542. With the success of his single Jingle Hell, Christopher Lee became the oldest musician to ever enter the billboard hot 100.

543. The song "Kickstart My Heart" was inspired by the death of Mötley Crüe bassist Nikki Sixx when he overdosed on heroin and the medical personnel had to bring him back to life. He was dead for 2 minutes.

544. The Beatles hold the record for most Rolling Stone magazine covers with more than 30.

545. While making 'Station to Station,' David Bowie's diet consisted of only red peppers, milk, and cocaine. He said that he does not even remember the recording sessions because he was so coked out

546. The Beatles holds the top spot of album sales in the United States as a band, with 178 million sold. They also hold the top spot for singles sales at 1.6 billion.

547. When Billy Idol's cover of Tommy James and the Shondells' song "Mony Mony" reached #1 on the charts in 1987, it dethroned Tiffany's "I Think We're Alone Now", which was also a cover of a Tommy James and the Shondells song.

548. The Beatles literally stopped touring because their music could not be amplified loud enough to compete with screaming crowd noise, even with custom, purpose-built amplifiers. Their last show was on August 29th, 1966 at Candlestick Park in San Francisco, California. This show ushered in the modern touring industry as we know it today.

549. The Beatles recorded "Strawberry Fields Forever" during the sessions for "Sgt. Pepper's Lonely Hearts Club Band" in the fall of 1966. The song was left off the album but appeared on 1968's "Magical Mystery Tour".

550. The Beatles song "Dear Prudence" was written about Mia Farrow's sister, Prudence, when she wouldn't come out and play with Mia and the Beatles at a religious retreat in India.

551. The Beatles used to be called "Johnny and the Moondogs".

552. The Beatles were turned down by every record label they approached.

553. Huey Lewis and the News considered calling themselves American Express, but their record label told them the name probably would not be appreciated by the credit card company. So, the band called themselves Huey Lewis and the News, a nod toward Lewis' passion for television news.

554. The Beatles wrote into their contracts for American concerts that they would not play in front of segregated audiences.

555. The Beatles' first album to debut at #1 was "Help".

556. The Black Sabbath song "Fairies Wear Boots" was inspired by an encounter with combat boot-wearing skinheads who disrupted one of the bands' early concerts.

557. The caricature of Anthrax used on their album "State of Euphoria" was created by Mad Magazine artist Mort Drucker.

558. The Carpenters signature song, "We've Only Just Begun," was originally part of a television commercial for a California bank.

559. The coughing heard at the beginning of "Sweet Leaf," off Black Sabbath's third studio album Master of Reality, is guitarist Tony Iommi. He had been smoking a joint in the studio given to him by Ozzy Osbourne. The title of the song was taken from a packet of Irish cigarettes which said, "It's the sweet leaf," and refers to marijuana, which the band was using frequently.

560. Queen is the only band in which every member has individually written more than one #1 hit.

561. The cover art for Obituary's "Cause of Death" album was originally intended for Sepultura's "Beneath the Remains" album.

562. The cover of Weezer's "Raditude" is a National Geographic photo.

563. Keith Richards snorted his father's ashes after he died in 2002. He mixed the ashes with cocaine.

564. The distinct horse logo that appeared on most of Poco's albums was designed by Saturday Night Live star, Phil Hartman.

565. Magne Furuholmen lost his father at age 5 in a plane crash outside of Oslo. The event was witnessed by 9 year old Morten Harket, thirteen years before the two would meet and form the band A-ha.

566. During a flight from Indianapolis, Indiana to Los Angeles, California, Guns N' Roses guitarist, Izzy Stradlin urinated in the isle of an airplane because he got tired of waiting for the bathroom to become free.

567. Phil Spector once held the Ramones at gunpoint and made them play "Baby, I Love You" repeatedly until 4:30am.

Rock and Roll Facts

568. Carlos Santana gives credit to a "mystical spirit" named Metatron for his "Supernatural" album not the producers, engineers and songwriters that made it happen.

569. Noodles, the guitarist in The Offspring was the school janitor and was welcomed into the band because he was old enough to buy alcohol.

570. Tommy Chong used to be in a band called Four n***ers and a Chink.

571. The Doors got their band name from the Aldous Huxley book, "The Doors of Perception".

572. The Doors turned down-playing at Woodstock because they thought it was going to be a "second class repeat of Monterey Pop festival".

573. The Doors were the first band to ever advertise their new album on a billboard.

574. The Eagles were originally the backup band for the singer Linda Ronstadt.

575. The famous Rolling Stone cover shot of a naked John Lennon curled against Yoko Ono was taken by Annie

Leibovitz at the same apartment complex and on the same day Lennon was fatally shot.

576. The fan who volunteered his face to be punched for Pantera's "Vulgar Display of Power" album cover had to withstand almost 80 punches before the final shot was chosen.

577. Freddie Mercury loved cats and he adopted most of his cats from rescue shelters. He gave them gourmet meals, Christmas stockings and talked to them over the phone when on tour.

578. The final song on Pink Floyd's album "Atom Heart Mother" - "Alan's Psychedelic Breakfast", features a dripping sink at the end where on original vinyl copies, the effect was cut into the vinyl's run-off groove, causing the dripping noise to play on infinitely until the stylus was removed.

579. The first album ever to receive Platinum certification from the Recording Industry Association of America was the Eagles' "Greatest Hits 1971 - 1975" on February 24th, 1976.

580. The first edition of Kerrang! Magazine was published in June 1981 and featured Angus Young of AC/DC on the cover.

581. The first group to be inducted into the Rock and Roll Hall of Fame were the 1958 configuration of The Coasters.

582. The first nationwide rock and roll hit was "Rock Around the Clock" by Bill Haley and His Comets. It debuted at #1 in 1955.

583. The first time Billy Joel played 'Just the Way You Are' for his then wife Elizabeth, she asked "Do I get the publishing too?" Billy would later say, "In retrospect, I probably should have known right then and there that the relationship was doomed. I had written 'Just the Way You Are' for someone who had changed."

584. John Lennon was once asked if he believed that Ringo Starr was the best drummer in the world. He said that Ringo wasn't even the best drummer in The Beatles.

585. The first time The Beatles smoked marijuana was with Bob Dylan. They met at a hotel and Dylan offered them some. Dylan assumed they had smoked before because he had misheard their "I can't hide" lyric from "I Want to Hold Your Hand" as "I get high".

586. The Goo Goo Dolls never thought "Iris" was going to be a hit since it was on the soundtrack to City of Angels alongside songs from bigger artists, like U2 and Alanis Morissette.

587. The guitar solo in The Beatle's "While My Guitar Gently Weeps" is played by Clapton.

588. The iconic line "Do you know where you are? You're in the jungle baby!", was actually yelled at Guns 'N' Roses singer Axl Rose, by a homeless man in New York.

589. The iconic rough timbre that Mick Jagger is known for, was altered from his posh voice, after he accidentally bit off part of his tongue while younger.

590. The Jimi Hendrix museum in Seattle, Washington was funded by Microsoft co-founder Paul Allen when he saw that Seattle had no shrine to Hendrix. The museum has now evolved into the Experience Music Project.

591. The largest free rock concert ever had 3.7 million people. It was held by Rod Stewart in Rio de Janeiro, Brazil.

592. The lead vocal of The Beach Boys' 1965, #1 hit, "Barbara Ann" was sung by Dean Torrence of Jan And Dean. Torrence was just hanging around the studio when everyone started to play the former Regents' hit, without knowing that the tape machine was still running.

593. The little boy seen on the cover of Ozzy Osbourne's "Diary of a Madman" is Ozzy's son Louis from his first marriage.

594. Jerry Lee Lewis once pulled a gun and demanded to see Elvis Presley.

595. The longest song to reach number one on the Billboard charts on LP was "I'd Do Anything for Love (But I Won't Do That)" by Meatloaf, the shortest: "Stay" by Maurice Williams and the Zodiacs.

596. The long-running, all-ages punk club often just called Gilman in Berkeley, California where Green Day got its start still exists, but Green Day have been banned from playing there since signing to a record label.

597. The members of Dream Theater all met when they all attended Berklee College of Music in Cambridge, Massachusetts.

598. Bruce Springsteen's E Street band took its name from an actual E Street located in Belmar, New Jersey. The keyboard player's mother lived on E Street, and she was happy to let the band rehearse there.

599. The moment John Lennon was pronounced dead a Beatles song came over the hospital's sound system.

600. The myth that Jimi Hendrix could not read or write music is false. He was very adept at the art of little black notes.

601. The Nelsons are the only family in history to have three generations that had a Billboard number one hit. Ozzie Nelson lead his orchestra to the top of the chart in 1932 with "And Then Some", Rick Nelson topped all others in 1961 with "Poor Little Fool" and "Travelin' Man", and Rick's sons, Gunnar and Matthew had a chart topper in 1990 with "Love & Affection".

602. The only guy without a beard in ZZ Top is Frank Beard.

603. The only time Elvis Presley and The Beatles met, the Fab Four were so starstruck that Elvis threatened to go to bed unless one of the band members spoke to him.

604. The opening line of "Layla" by Eric Clapton, is Duane Allman playing guitar.

605. The orchestral strings on R.E.M.'s "Automatic for the People" were arranged by John Paul Jones of Led Zeppelin.

606. The original album cover for AC/DCs "Highway to Hell" is purported to have been the devil driving a car, peering in his rear view mirror, with the band all seated in the back seat. A photoshoot was even conducted in Staten Island, NY, which featured the band hitchhiking. In the end the record company baulked at the idea, instead using a shot from the "Powerage" shoot, super-imposing horns, and a satanic tail on Angus. One of the new shots was used on the back cover.

607. The original Eagles, Glen Frey, Don Henley, Randy Meisner and Bernie Leadon first met when they were members of Linda Ronstadt's touring band.

608. The origins of Nickelback's name came from bassist Mike Kroeger as he toiled in Starbucks, repeating the same mantra as he handed customers their change: "here's your nickel back".

609. The P.M.R.C. (Parent's Music Resource Committee), led by Tipper Gore, does more to help album sales than hinder them. Albums with a "PMRC" sticker on it advising that it has restricted content such as suggestive lyrics or violent content, helps the album sell more copies.

610. The phrase "Teenage Idol" was first used by Time magazine to describe 16 year old Rick Nelson in the cover story of their December 1958 issue. Nelson would release a song called "Teenage Idol" in July of 1962 that would reach number 5 in the U.S.

611. Bon Jovi named their second album 4800 Fahrenheit after Fahrenheit 451, a novel by Ray Bradbury. 451 degrees is the temperature at which books will catch on fire, and 4800 degrees is the temperature at which rocks melt. The band wanted the title of the 1985 album to connote "American hot rock."

612. The piano Freddie Mercury plays on "Bohemian Rhapsody" is the exact same piano Paul McCartney played on "Hey Jude".

613. The piano player on Simon And Garfunkel's "Bridge Over Troubled Water" is Larry Knechtel, who later joined the Soft Rock group Bread.

614. Bachman Turner Overdrive was rejected by 25 record companies before they were signed by Mercury Records.

615. The producer recording "Sweet Child O' Mine" with Guns n' Roses suggested there be a breakdown at the end of the song. The band had no idea where to take the song, resulting in the iconic repetition of "Where do we go now?"

616. The real name of AC/DC's Bon Scott is Ronald Belford Scott. But after moving to Australia from Scotland, people made fun of him by calling him Bonnie Scotland. Later he shortened it and kept his name Bon Scott.

617. The real name of each original member of KISS is Chaim Witz (Gene Simmons), Stanley Eisen (Paul Stanley), Paul Frehley (Ace Frehley) and George Criscuola (Peter Criss).

618. The Rolling Stones got their first taste of "Tequila Sunrise," in a private party in Sausalito, California, following which the band ordered the same during their shows. The members even went on to give pointers to bartenders while preparing the drinks, leading "Tequila Sunrise's" popularity.

619. The Rolling Stones got their name from one of their major influences, Muddy Waters and his most famous tune "Rollin' Stone Blues."

620. Actor Tim Curry was an avid horticulturist and he even planted a garden for his friend Freddie Mercury.

621. The Rolling Stones played a private concert for a fee of $7 million for the Texas investor named David Bonderman in 2002.

622. Iron Maiden's song "Rime of the Ancient Mariner", from their 1984 album "Powerslave", is based on an 18th century poem of the same name written by Samuel Taylor Coleridge.

623. The Rolling Stones were criticized for high ticket prices on their 1969 U.S. tour, so they decided to hold a free concert. The festival was organized by the Grateful Dead and took place at the Altamont Speedway in 1969. It turned fatal when a Hell's Angel stabbed and killed a young black concertgoer. It was a disaster and signaled the end of the hippie movement.

624. The Rolling Stones were so impressed with the backup singer's voice in "Gimme Shelter" that you can hear them hooting in the background. They kept it in the studio recording as well.

625. Steve Vai's design Jem guitar is one of the most successful signature guitar series in history.

626. The Rolling Stones would never have been formed if Keith Richards and Mick Jagger had not accidentally met at a train station in 1961. Richards struck up a conversation with Jagger about the blues records that he was carrying. The connection was instant, and the rest is history.

627. The Rolling Stones' 1981 world tour was the first tour ever to be sponsored. It is reported that Jovan perfume paid them $4 million as sponsor.

628. The second floor of Elvis Presley's Graceland is forbidden and the only non-family member to see it was Nicholas Cage, who was married to Lisa Marie Presley.

629. The sex noises in "Rocket Queen" by Guns N' Roses were real and were made by Axl Rose having sex with drummer Steven Adler's girlfriend in the studio.

630. The song "Black Dog" got its name after a Black Labrador roamed into the studio during a Led Zeppelin recording session.

631. The 1967 movie "Barbarella" featured a quirky character called Dr. Durand Durand. The band Duran Duran performed their first music gigs in 1978 at a club whose name was Barbarella's, and the group named themselves after the character in the movie.

632. Slash from Guns N' Roses once had a pet mountain lion named Curtis that he would take on tour with him.

633. The song "Purple Haze" was written by Jimi Hendrix after he had a dream about walking underwater.

634. The song "You Oughta Know" by Alanis Morrisette, features Dave Navarro and Flea from the Red Hot Chili Peppers on guitar and bass, respectively.

635. The Stuxnet virus, which was the virus that shut down the Iran's nuclear plants, made emergency speakers blast "Thunderstruck" by AC/DC before shutting down all systems.

636. The title track of Megadeth's "Countdown to Extinction" album was awarded the Humane Society's Genesis Award in 1993 for raising awareness about animal rights.

637. The US military would play Enter Sandman for hours on end to aid in the interrogation and torture of prisoners. When asked about this, Metallica's James Hetfield responded "We've been punishing our parents, our wives, our loved ones with this music forever. Why should the Iraqis be any different?"

638. Steven Tyler once convinced the parents of a 14 year-old girl to sign over custody to him in 1975.

639. The Van Halen brothers were born in the Netherlands and trained as concert pianists. The name of the band was originally Mammoth.

640. After Dave Grohl left his first band, they decided to quit because they knew they would never find a drummer as good as him.

641. There is a statue of Freddie Mercury in Switzerland.

642. The Verve had to sign away 100% of their royalties for "Bitter Sweet Symphony" to Mick Jagger, Keith Richards, and former Rolling Stones manager Allen Klein after they sampled more notes than they had originally agreed upon from an obscure orchestral recording of the Stones' "The Last Time."

643. The very first CD available for commercial release was Billy Joel's "52nd Street", issued in Japan in 1982. The first CD pressed in the United States for commercial release was Bruce Springsteen's "Born in the USA".

644. The video for Nine Inch Nails iconic' "Closer" video was filmed with a vintage camera from 1919 that had to be hand-cranked.

645. The voice actors for SpongeBob and Karen Plankton, Tom Kenny, and Jill Talley, play the couple that travel to the moon in the music video for the Smashing Pumpkins' "Tonight, Tonight." They are also married in real life.

646. The Who's 1976 hit "Squeeze Box" was originally intended to be introduced on a television special planned in 1974. In the performance of the song, the members of the band were to have been surrounded by 100 topless women playing accordions as they played the song. The performance never happened.

647. The Who's drummer Keith Moon washed down some horse tranquilizers with brandy before a show, then drummed slower and slower until he passed out while playing "Won't Get Fooled Again."

648. David Bowie once kept a four-foot-deep, fur-covered bed nicknamed "the pit" in his living room for orgies with famous friends.

649. Freddie Mercury used a piano as a headboard for his bed and taught himself to play the piano backwards so if a song idea popped into his head when lying in bed, he could reach backwards and play it or record it.

650. There are unreleased recordings of The Beatles rehearsing for a show in Germany, complete with them singing "Get Back" in German and playing traditional blues songs.

651. There is a metal band called Hatebeak whose lead singer is an African grey parrot.

652. There is a Swedish Speed Metal band called "Sabaton" that teaches history through its music, including an album devoted to teaching about World War 2.

653. There was a female Rock Band name 'Rockbitch' which was famous for throwing 'Golden Condoms' at their audience and whoever got it, male or female, was taken backstage to have sex with band members.

654. There was some controversy to the inclusion of Chuck Berry's 'Johnny B. Goode' on the Voyager Golden Record. Carl Sagan was told that rock music was adolescent. Sagan responded, "There are a lot of adolescents on the planet."

655. Third Eye Blind's "Jumper" is a about a gay man who jumped off a bridge after being bullied.

656. Throughout their career, Ringo received far more fan mail than any of the other Beatles.

657. Ian Gillam of Deep Purple was the original Jesus Christ in the rock opera Jesus Christ Superstar. He was selected by the authors of the rock opera, Andrew Lloyd Webber, and Tim Rice.

658. Tom Morello of Rage Against the Machine earned a Bachelor of Arts degree in Social Studies at Harvard University.

659. Tom Petty was so popular his record label wanted to charge $1 more for his 1981 album "Hard Promises" than the standard $8.98, but they backed down after he considered naming the album "$8.98".

660. Tool guitarist Adam Jones worked at special effects studios designing creatures for major motion pictures such as "Jurassic Park", "Terminator 2" and "A Nightmare on Elm Street".

661. Tool singer Maynard James Keenan served in the U.S. Army and has studied Jiu-Jitsu with Brazilian martial arts legend Rickson Gracie.

662. Tool's 2001 song "Mantra" consists basically of a slowed-down recording of singer Maynard James Keenan squeezing his cat.

663. Trent Reznor felt his song "A Warm Place" was too good to be his own work. After the song had been released, he was horrified to discover that he had indeed copied the melody from a piece by David Bowie called "Crystal Japan", written for a Japanese gin advertisement. Bowie found this hilarious.

664. U2 was originally known as Feedback. U2 have sold more than 70 million records.

665. U2 front man Bono got his name from a hearing aid store in the center of Dublin, where he grew up. His previous pseudonyms were "Bonavox of O'Connell Street," "Bonavox," "Bono Vox" and originally "Steinhegvanhuysenolegbangbangbang."

666. Kiss guitarist Paul Stanley was born without any hearing in his right ear and has had to wear an implanted hearing aid most of his life. He was born with Level 3 Microtia, a deformity of the cartilage of the outer ear.

667. U2's "Sunday Bloody Sunday" originally started with the phrase "Don't talk to me about the rights of the IRA" but was ultimately changed to "I can't believe the news today" because U2 was afraid that their peace calling would be misunderstood.

668. Until 2006, U2 paid no tax in Ireland due to an exemption for artists. When the exemption was capped at $315,000, the band moved its accounts to the Netherlands, rather than face a multi-million dollar tax bill for album sales and royalties.

669. Until she was 8 years old, Liv Tyler thought Todd Rundgren was her biological father. Turns out it was Steven Tyler of Aerosmith.

670. Van Halen would always put a "no brown M&Ms" in their touring contracts. The reason for this was to see if the promoters were really reading the contracts. If they found brown M&Ms they would trash the backstage area.

671. W.A.S.P.'s Blackie Lawless briefly appears in "This is Spinal Tap" during the "sex farm" portion of the movie's closing infomercial.

672. Weezer's first show was opening for Keanu Reeves' band Dogstar in 1992.

673. Freddie Mercury had a degree in art and graphic design, and he designed the Queen's logo, called the Queen Crest.

674. Weird Al Yankovic has asked permission from Prince to parody his songs on numerous occasions and has always been refused. When the two were assigned to sit in the same row at an award's show, he got a telegram from Prince's lawyers demanding that he not make eye contact.

675. When "Creep" was released in 1992, it was not a success. When Radiohead released it again the next year it was an international hit.

676. When AC/DC singer Bon Scott sent out his Christmas cards in 1979, something he did every year, he didn't pay enough

postage, meaning many of the cards were delayed and arrived late, after he had died on February 19, 1980.

677. When David Bowie played his song "Andy Warhol" to Andy Warhol, he did not like it. When the song had finished playing, Warhol and Bowie reportedly just stared at each other for a while until Warhol said, "I like your shoes" and the pair then had a conversation about shoes.

678. When Agnostic Front guitarist Vinnie Stigma launched himself off a bandmate's shoulders, he nearly scalped himself on the speakers overhead. He was rushed to the hospital so doctors could reattach his skin to his exposed skull.

679. When asked if there was validity in the media's criticism of violence in his movies, Quentin Tarantino said, "Sure, Kill Bill's a violent movie. But it's a Tarantino movie. You don't go to see Metallica and ask the f*ckers to turn the music down."

680. When Dave Grohl joined Nirvana, he was the 5th person to get behind a drumkit for the band. He auditioned after his previous band (Scream) disbanded.

681. When Davie Bowie heard Nirvana's cover of "The Man Who Sold the World", he said he was "blown away" by the fact Kurt Cobain liked his work and said "it would have been nice to have worked with him, but just talking with him would

have been real cool".

682. When Decca Records first released "Rock Around the Clock" by Bill Haley and His Comets in the Spring of 1954, most people had never heard of Rock and Roll and the company had a hard time describing the song. The label on the single called it a "Novelty Foxtrot."

683. When disc jockey Alan Freed heard the song "My Baby Rocks Me with a Steady Roll", he coined the term "rock and roll" in 1951 while working for radio station WJW in Cleveland, Ohio.

684. When Elvis Presley was 4 years old, a tornado hit Tupelo, Mississippi and destroyed most of the homes around the Presley's. When a young Elvis asked his mother Gladys why their house was not destroyed, she said to him "because God has big plans for you.

685. When Elvis Presley was discharged from the Army on March 5th, 1960, RCA Records wasted no time in getting him back into the recording studio. Anticipation for the new Elvis single was so great, the record company had taken 1,275,077 orders for the un-released song, making "Stuck on You" a million seller before it was even recorded.

686. When Freddie Mercury died on November 24th, 1991 at the age of 45, his close friend, Dave Clark of The Dave Clark Five, was at his bedside.

Rock and Roll Facts

687. When given a choice of birthday gifts as a child, Pantera guitarist asked his parents for a BMX bike instead of a guitar.

688. When Grateful Dead singer Jerry Garcia died, an autopsy was done. In his large intestine, the medical examiner found a bottle cap, a pipe screen, a mascara brush, and a small brass key "probably consumed in Buffalo, between 1979 and 1981."

689. Elvis and his entourage used to rent roller skating rinks to throw fireworks worth $15,000 at each other. This astonishing play included air force jumpsuits, gloves, helmets, and goggles as their attire.

690. Freddie Mercury hated doing Bohemian Rhapsody live because he considered himself a mediocre pianist.

691. When Guns n' Roses guitarist Slash was 8 years old, he walked in on his mother and David Bowie naked in bed together.

692. When Janis Joplin was in college in 1963, a local fraternity voted her "The Ugliest Man on Campus."

693. When John Lennon was asked if Ringo Starr was the best drummer in the world he replied "In the world? He`s not even the best drummer in The Beatles!".

694. When Marilyn Manson was 11 years old, his father Hugh Warner dressed up as KISS bassist Gene Simmons before escorting his son to see KISS live.

695. When Motorhead's Lemmy tried to follow Keith Richards' lead and get his blood purified, the doctors refused. They told him his blood was so toxic with drugs that normal blood would probably kill him.

696. When Ozzy Osbourne hired a dwarf to cavort with him onstage, he nicked named him Ronnie as a dig against the diminutive vocalist for Black Sabbath rival, Ronnie James Dio.

697. When Pearl Jam released their cover of 'Last Kiss' as a single, they decided all proceeds would go to Kosovo War refugees. The song raised ten million dollars.

698. Freddie Mercury's powerful voice spanned over a four-octave range.

699. When Pink Floyd was completing "Shine on You Crazy Diamond," which was an exploration of their former band mate Syd Barrett's mental decline, an overweight man with a shaved head and eyebrows entered the studio. He turned out to be Syd Barrett himself, who they had not seen in 7 years.

700. When Prince was a kid, his dad put him onstage with James Brown and he danced with him until security pulled him off.

701. The baby noises heard in "Magic Dance" in The Labyrinth were dubbed over by David Bowie himself because he felt the actual baby did not perform as required.

702. When Queen wanted to release "Bohemian Rhapsody", various executives told them that a song with a length of 5 minutes and 55 seconds was too long and would never be a hit. They even played it to other musicians who claimed that the song had "no hope" of being played on the radio.

703. When Queen wanted to release "Bohemian Rhapsody", various executives told them that a song with a length of 5 minutes and 55 seconds was too long and would never be a hit. They even played it to other musicians who claimed that the song had "no hope" of being played on the radio.

704. When Quincy Jones called to ask Eddie Van Halen to do the guitar solo on Michael Jackson's "Beat It", Van Halen thought it was a prank call and called Jones an a*shole before hanging up on him.

705. When Ringo Starr's 1963 Ludwig drum kit was sold at an auction in December 2015, it was the first time they had been seen in public in over fifty years.

706. When Sam Philips' brother, Jud Philips, tried to get an audition for Jerry Lee Lewis on The Ed Sullivan Show in July 1957, Sullivan told him, "Get out of here. I don't want any more of this Elvis junk."

707. When Steve Winwood left the Spencer Davis Group in the summer of 1967, one of the rejected applicants to be auditioned was a young piano player named Reginald Dwight, who would later launch a solo career, re-naming himself, Elton John.

708. When the Arctic Monkeys started their band, none of them could play instruments.

709. When The Beach Boys album "That's Why God Made the Radio" peaked at #3 in the Summer of 2012, it became the band's first Top Ten LP of original material in 49 years.

710. When the Offspring's early drummer James Lilja left the band, he retrained as a gynecologist.

711. When thrash metal band Overkill noticed the similarity between their mascot and Avenged Sevenfold's, they made shirts that read "Get your own f**cking logo".

712. When University of Vienna students were asked their reasons behind choosing to learn Finnish, 97% of respondents said the main factor behind their decision was heavy metal music.

713. When Weird Al Yankovic did a parody of Nirvana's song, "Smells Like Teen Spirit," (which is called "Smells Like Nirvana") Nirvana's lead singer Kurt Cobain considered the parody as a sign that they had "made it" as a band.

714. While awaiting trial on narcotics charges in 1967, Keith Richards took a road trip from London to Morocco (via ferry). He left town in a custom Bentley that he dubbed "Blue Lena," after singer Lena Horne, that had a secret compartment for hiding drugs.

715. While on tour in Brazil to promote its new album Omen, the band Antestor was attacked by Satanist black metal fans angered by the Christian beliefs of the band members.

716. While still known as Reg Dwight, Elton John was paid 12 Pounds to play piano on The Hollies' 1969 hit, "He Ain't Heavy, He's My Brother".

717. While the song was still under development, the first working title of what would become The Eagles "Hotel California" was "Mexican Reggae".

718. William Bailey is the real name of musician Axl Rose. Axl Rose is an anagram for oral sex.

719. David Bowie was next on a hit list of targets of John Lennon's assassin, Mark David Chapman.

720. Woodstock Ventures, the sponsors of the original Woodstock Festival, lost more than $1.2 million on the concert.

721. Worried that no one would understand their Liverpool accents in the 1964 film "A Hard Day's Night", U.S. music executives considered dubbing them with American actors. McCartney replied, "We can understand a f**cking cowboy talking Texan!"

722. Yoko Ono once brought a dead rat in a shoe box to a recording studio and insisted that the sound engineer record it. The engineer recorded two takes of the "dead rat solo."

723. ZZ Top has had the same members without any changes since 1969.

724. The Moonwalk pre-dates Michael Jackson by at least 50 years, having been performed by James Brown, David Bowie, Dick Van Dyke and Cab Calloway.

725. Rod Stewart's aggressive blues work with The Jeff Beck Group and the Faces influenced the heavy metal genre.

726. Nikki Sixx and Tommy Lee from Mötley Crüe decided to wager a bet in 1980 while sitting in a hot tub to see who could go the longest without showering or bathing. After months had gone by, neither of them had gave in. That was until Nikki Sixx was receiving oral sex from a female fan who got so nauseated and sick, she ended up throwing up her spaghetti dinner in his crotch.

727. Gene Simmons of KISS has reportedly slept with over 4,000 women and has photo albums filled with pictures of each one.

728. "Pour Some Sugar on Me" is one of Def Leppard's greatest hits, reaching the top of the Billboard Hot 100 in 1988 and remaining on the charts for 24 weeks. Lead singer Joe Elliott got the idea for the song at his home in London when he asked his producer, Mutt Lange, for sugar for his tea. Lange asked whether he wanted one or two lumps, and Elliott replied, "I don't care. Just pour some sugar on me."

729. Rod Stewart used cocaine anally to avoid nasal damage.

Rock and Roll Facts

730. Captain Beefheart ran his band like a religious cult, exercising terrifying levels of control over their emotions and creative input, and feeding them a cup of soybeans a day for eight months of solid rehearsing. Drummer John French recalled how he was "screamed at, beaten up, drugged, ridiculed, humiliated, arrested, starved, stolen from, and thrown down a half-flight of stairs" by Beefheart.

731. Steven Tyler of Aerosmith claims he has spent over $6 million dollars on drugs.

732. In 1991, Per Yngve "Dead" Ohlin lived up to his stage-name and committed suicide by shooting himself in the head with a shotgun. His Monty Python-esque suicide note simply read: "sorry about the mess". Finding Dead's body, his bandmates removed fragments of skull to make necklaces, made lumps of gore into a broth that they ate, and took photographs of the carnage. One of these bloody images became the cover art for a bootleg live album, "Dawn of the Black Hearts".

733. On stage in 1965, The Kinks' drummer knocked out Kinks guitarist Dave Davies with a cymbal stand.

734. GG Allin (real name Jesus Christ Allin), was arrested 52 times for his onstage antics. Many of which were defecating on stage. Eating his own feces. Cutting himself and inserting items into his rectum.

735. In a now-infamous incident, Guns N' Roses frontman Axl Rose became enraged when he spotted an unauthorized camera in the front row at a show in St. Louis, MO. When security guards failed to confiscate the camera, Rose took it upon himself to handle the situation. "I'll take it, goddamnit!" he exclaimed before punching the man in the face. He left the stage, and a three-hour riot broke out, before Rose was ultimately arrested and charged with assault. Guns N' Roses were also banned for life from the city.

736. During a 2001 performance in Michigan, Marilyn Manson grabbed a security guard named Joshua Keasler from behind and used him as a human stripper pole. Manson spit on Keasler and rubbed his genitals on the security guard's head. The singer was arrested and charged with misdemeanor assault and battery, as well as criminal sexual conduct. The sexual conduct charge was ultimately reduced, and the singer was not required to face jail time as the original charge would have mandated.

737. In 1965 three of the five members of the Rolling Stones - Mick Jagger, Brian Jones, and Bill Wyman - stopped at a gas station in East Ham, United Kingdom, to use the bathroom. The attendant at the gas station refused to let them use the bathroom because he didn't like their long-haired appearance, prompting Jagger to respond with now-infamous words, "We'll piss anywhere, man," Jagger responded before Wyman did just that and urinated on the wall. All three were arrested and hit with a small fine.

738. A used-car salesman offered Zappa, who was surrounded by go-go dancers during his performance, $100 to record audio of himself having sex. With the help of a dancer named Lorraine Belcher, Zappa created a fake audio sex tape - later recalling that he "stayed up most of the night manufacturing this bogus sex tape, fake bedsprings, squeaks, and grunts." Before he could hand over the tape, he was arrested, along with Belcher. He posted bail for the dancer but could not afford defense for himself, so he pleaded guilty and served 10 days in jail on a six-month suspended sentence.

739. Dave Navarro of Jane's Addiction and Red Hot Chili Peppers was escorted out of the Playboy mansion and asked to never return after he was caught on video squirting blood on the walls of the "orgy room" with a syringe with 3 naked girls at his feet.

740. There is only one line in Pink Floyd's "One of These Days." Nick Mason, the drummer recorded the line, "One of these days, I'm going to cut you into little pieces." That is the only line he ever sang on a Pink Floyd album. He is also the only member to play on every Pink Floyd album.

741. Led Zeppelin's song "D'yer Mak'er" is a humorous take on the word "Jamaica" which is why the song has a bit of a Reggae feel to it.

742. Jimi Hendrix got his first guitar for $5. It was an acoustic.

743. Nirvana turned down offers to tour with Guns N' Roses and U2 because those bands were too mainstream.

744. In the 1960s, Fats Domino had 11 top ten hits. Only Elvis Presley sold more albums.

745. As a child, Ronnie James Dio learned the trumpet and his father made him have lessons for two hours every day. He played trumpet on stage with Gene Pitney when he was 15.

746. Hard Rock Cafe was started by two Americans, Isaac Tigrett and Peter Morton, who were living in London and could not find a good American burger in the city. Hard Rock's music memorabilia collection began in 1979 when Eric Clapton, a regular at the London restaurant, donated his red Fender Leader II guitar. He asked the staff to hang the guitar over his usual seat, which then prompted Pete Townshend of The Who to give the staff one of his guitars to hang with a note saying: "Mine's as good as his! Love, Pete."

747. The keyboard used by Tommy Lee of Mötley Crüe on their song "Home Sweet Home" for their live album was provided to Tommy by the author of this book.

748. James Hetfield wrote Metallica's song "Fade to Black" about the loss of his favorite Marshall amp head.

749. It is so hard to understand the words to The Kingmen's famous rendition of "Louie Louie" that kids used to make up their own versions of the lyrics and pass them around in notes. There were so many suspicious parents reporting it for being obscene that the F.B.I. began an investigation. They spent over 2.5 years playing the song backwards and forwards, but they eventually gave up after determining the words were "indecipherable at any speed."

750. KISS has never had a #1 hit.

751. Freddie Mercury of Queen wrote "Crazy Little Thing Called Love" in a bathtub at a hotel. He got inspiration and had the piano brought to his tub to allow him to compose.

752. Classic rock is voted the favorite genre among age groups spanning 35-65+, and almost half (49%) of 25-34 consider it their favorite.

753. After more than 50 years on the music scene, The Rolling Stones (average age 73) made the most money per show performed in 2016: $91 million from just 14 concerts.

754. The symbol of the band KISS must be altered in countries like Germany and Israel where the double lightning bolt, which was used by Hitler and the Nazis, are banned.

755. The Police got their band name from drummer Stewart Copeland. His father worked for the C.I.A.

756. "867-5309/Jenny", recorded by Tommy Tutone, was released in 1983, and it immediately gave rise to a tremendous number of crank calls to people who had 867-5309 as their phone number. The Jenny phenomenon was still in evidence 21 years later in 2004, when a New Jersey disc jockey requested the number, thinking it would go well with his business, only to find himself inundated by calls and messages.

757. Since they became famous during hair metal's height of popularity, Twisted Sister is often considered glam metal, but they rejected the label, considering themselves to be a parody of a glam metal band. Lead singer Dee Snider once made the comment that he rejected the "glam" label because it meant "glamour" and that Twisted Sister should be referred to as "hid" since they were "hideous."

758. Mötley Crüe's first music gig at the Troubador in 1981 was extraordinarily successful and broke attendance records for the club. Van Halen's David Lee Roth saw the show and gave them some good, solid advice about how to succeed in the music industry.

759. One of Guns N Roses' biggest hits, "Sweet Child o' Mine", was written in only five minutes. Duff McKagan, the bass guitarist, is quoted as saying it was a three chord song that was the result of Slash, the lead guitarist, just "messing around." Slash was quoted as saying that "Sweet Child o' Mine" was his least favorite of all the band's songs, but fans loved it. The song hit number one on the Billboard Hot 100 and stayed on the charts for 24 weeks.

760. Davey Jones of The Monkees used to be a horse jockey.

761. Randy Bachman was a member of the Guess Who but left at the height of their popularity due to his religious beliefs and formed Bachman Turner Overdrive.

762. Keith Moon, legendary drummer for The Who, was not quite as good on the mic as he was with the drums. The band barred him from the studio whenever vocals were being recorded.

763. At ZZ Top's first show in Alvin, Texas there was only one person. He still attends as many ZZ Top shows that he can. He will not tell the band his name.

764. Elvis' Hound Dog took 31 takes to record.

765. None of The Beatles play on Eleanor Rigby. Aside from vocals, the song was performed entirely by studio musicians.

766. Jerry Garcia of the Grateful Dead played several types of music, including folk, bluegrass, country, rock 'n' roll, and acid rock. In fact, Garcia performed in a country band, New Riders of the Purple Sage, which opened for the Grateful Dead for several concerts.

767. The first time Led Zeppelin played "Stairway to Heaven" live, the audience booed.

768. Jim Morrison, lead singer of the Doors, was sentenced to eight months of hard labor and a $500 fine in 1970 for indecent exposure and using profanity during a concert in Florida. He appealed the sentence but died before his legal issues were resolved.

769. Eric Clapton penned the song Wonderful Tonight while waiting for his then wife Patti Boyd Harrison, who had been previously married to close Clapton friend George Harrison, to get ready for a party at Paul and Linda McCartney's house. The party was their annual homage to Buddy Holly.

770. The common phrase "life in the fast lane" was first introduced into popular language and culture by the Eagles' song of the same name.

771. Foghat is named after a fake word made up by the band's singer Dave Peverett and his brother during a game of Scrabble.

772. In 1964, 60 percent of the records sold in the U.S. were Beatles records.

773. As the track "All You Need is Love" by The Beatles, descends into calamity at the end, a brief snippet from the vocal melody of another Beatles single, She Loves You, can be heard. Other songs, including Greensleeves, Glenn Miller's "In the Mood" and a piece by J.S. Bach are also referenced.

774. KORN guitarist, Brian "Head" Welch, became a born-again Christian.

775. When Max Yasgur, the middle-aged, blue-collar farmer that owned the land that allowed Woodstock to take place on his property for a fee of $50,000 addressed the massive audience, he received as loud an ovation as Jimi Hendrix.

776. Guns N' Roses originally considered the names "Heads of Amazon" and "AIDS" for band names.

777. Steve Vai played for Alcatraz, Frank Zappa, David Lee Roth and Whitesnake.

778. Peter Tork was recommended for The Monkees by Stephen Stills.

779. The band Ugly Kid Joe got its name in response to the band Pretty Boy Floyd.

780. On June 3rd, 1956, authorities in Santa Cruz, California announced a total ban on rock and roll at public gatherings, calling the music "Detrimental to both the health and morals of our youth and community.".

781. Jack White of The White Stripes was accepted to the Wisconsin Seminary and almost pursued the life of a priest.

782. Steve Vai played for Alcatraz, Frank Zappa, David Lee Roth and Whitesnake.

783. "Back in Black" by AC/DC was the first song Kurt Cobain of Nirvana learned how to play on guitar.

784. At the beginning of "Roxanne" by The Police, you can hear Sting laughing. He had just tripped over a keyboard in the studio while the band were recording the song. They liked it and kept it in the track.

785. Florence Welch of Florence and the Machine used to sing at funerals as a child.

786. Def Leppard's first show was in 1978 in a high school gymnasium in their hometown of Sheffield, England. Only 6 people showed up in the audience.

787. The Beatles earned $90,000 in 35 minutes for their Minneapolis show in August 1965.

788. During the filming of the video "Eyes Without a Face", Billy Idol's contact lenses dried out so badly that they nearly fussed to his corneas.

789. Marilyn Manson has rules for a woman to have sex with him: The lights will remain off. He will rarely step out of his underwear in case of a quick getaway, he likes to have sex 5 times per day and his favorite place to have sex is in an antique abortionist's chair covered in a bearskin rug.

Rock and Roll Facts

790. While guesting at a popular music camp, singer Brian Wilson of The Beach Boys stepped onstage and proceeded to fall backwards over a stage monitor.

791. Lynyrd Skynyrd is the only rock back with a 13 letter name that does not contain any vowels.

792. In 1971, The Rolling Stones filled up a kiddie pool with Cap'n Crunch cereal and KY Jelly. Then as Keith Richards said "Maybe some groupies rolled around in it. I don't know. I went to sleep."

793. Over 1,000,000 copies of the sheet music for "Stairway to Heaven" have been sold. For most popular songs, the number is usually between 10,000-15,000.

794. When Freddie Mercury originally wrote "Bohemian Rhapsody", he called it "The Cowboy Song" because of its western feel.

795. Mötley Crüe used to rub egg burritos on their penises so their girlfriends would not smell the sex they had with other women.

796. Sebastian Bach of Skid Row is the voice of Triton of SpongeBob Squarepants.

797. Motorhead released 22 studio albums, 10 live recordings, 12 compilations and 5 EPs over their 40 active years as a band.

798. At the pleading of a publisher, and with the promise of a $1 million advance, Jagger wrote his autobiography in 1980, but ultimately decided not to publish that, or any other autobiography. British journalist John Blake claims to own the only copy of Jagger's 75,000-word manuscript.

799. Izzy Stradlin of Guns N' Roses name is a play on Easy Straddling.

800. John Lennon said the only true songs he ever wrote were "Help!" and "Strawberry Fields Forever." He says they were the only songs he wrote from experience and not by projecting himself into a situation and "writing a nice little story about it."

801. Dave Grohl of Foo Fighters worked with Jack Black on Tenacious D's debut album. You can see him playing Satan in their video for "Tribute". They teamed up again in 2006 for the film "Tenacious D in The Pick of Destiny", where Grohl played Beelzeboss and contributed to the soundtrack.

802. The original name of Black Sabbath was The Polka Tulk Blues Band. At the time, they had a slide guitar player and a

saxophonist. They then changed it to Earth and eventually Black Sabbath.

803. Ozzy Osbourne suffers from dyslexia.

804. Mick Jagger secretly paid the funeral costs for blues guitarist Hubert Sumlin after his death in 2011.

805. Geezer Butler of Black Sabbath once pulled a knife on Malcolm Young of AC/DC when they were on tour together.

806. Over the course of a single Rolling Stones show, Mick Jagger walks an estimated 12 miles.

807. Frank Sinatra described the Beatles song "Something" as the greatest love song ever written.

808. George Harrison's song "Blue Jay Way" has led to the repeated theft of that street sign in Los Angeles. The song was written at a house on Blue Jay Way in the Hollywood Hills.

809. The original members of AC/DC were Malcolm Young, brother Angus, Dave Evans on vocals, Colin Burgess on drums and bassist Larry Van Kriedt.

810. On tour, Metallica had pink backstage passes that have a smiley face on them. They would give these passes to women that gave oral sex.

811. On more than one occasion, Elvis Presley lent Buddy Holly his own personal guitar to use for his performances when Buddy opened a series of shows for Elvis in 1955.

812. The original Woodstock site is now on the National Register of Historic Places.

813. David Lee Roth called his penis "Little Elvis".

814. The founder of the "Hotel California" the Eagles sang about was a Chinese immigrant named Mr. Wong. He changed his name to Don Antonio Tabasco, wanting locals to believe he was Mexican.

815. MCA Records did not want to include Lynyrd Skynyrd's song "Free Bird" on the band's first album; they thought it was too long for radio stations to play.

816. The Rolling Stones put "Start Me Up" on the back burner for 4 years before adding it to an album; they could not find a good beat to match the lyrics.

817. "Rocket 88" by Ike Turner is the first rock and roll single. It was written by Ike Turner and sung by Jackie Brenston.

818. "Back in Black" by AC/DC is a tribute to their previous singer Bon Scott who "died of misadventure" after a night of partying.

819. All four members of The Beatles contracted gonorrhea in Hamburg, Germany early in their career.

820. The Ramones never talked onstage, other than counting the song in.

821. Cream recorded just two full studio albums and were together for barely two years.

822. During the making of Marillion's album "Misplaced Childhood", which was recorded in Berlin, Germany at Hansa Studios, singer Fish threw bricks over the Berlin Wall in an attempt to set off landmines.

823. The original site of Woodstock was intended to be at Howard Mills Industrial Park in Wallkill, near Middletown, New York. The residents feared the town would be inundated with visitors under the influence of alcohol and drugs. By insisting the concert's portable toilets were not up to code and refusing to grant a permit, Wallkill effectively banned Woodstock from taking place there just a month before its scheduled August 15th start date.

824. When Jerry Leiber and Mike Stoller met Elvis Presley in 1954 at the age of 21, they were astonished at his encyclopedic understanding of the blues.

825. Rolling Stone readers voted Nirvana one of the worst bands of the 1990's, along with Creed, Limp Bizkit and Hanson.

826. When Vaclav Havel got into power, he asked Frank Zappa to be the Czech Minister of Culture. Frank Zappa was an idol to the Czech underground and became firm friends with Havel although he declined the post.

827. In the 1980s, the Sunset Strip in Hollywood, California, became the epicenter of glam metal with bands like Mötley Crüe, Poison, RATT, Quiet Riot, and later Guns N' Roses dominating the musical landscape.

828. In 1967, The Monkees sold more albums than The Beatles and The Rolling Stones combined.

829. Axl Rose of Guns N' Roses filled in for Brian Johnson of AC/DC when Johnson was deemed medically unfit to tour due to hearing issues.

830. John Lennon's eyesight was so poor that he was legally blind without his glasses.

831. Gene Simmons of KISS can speak Hungarian.

832. "Peggy Sue" by Buddy Holly was originally going to be named "Cindy Lou" as a nod to Buddy's niece, Cindy Lou Kaiter. However, Jerry Allison, Holly's drummer, convinced Holly to name a song after his girlfriend Peggy Sue Gerron.

833. Tracii Guns of L.A. Guns was the original guitarist in Guns N' Roses. The band got its name from Axl Rose and Tracii Guns.

834. It is estimated that Mick Jagger has slept with over 4,000 women including Angelina Jolie and Carly Simon.

835. The Arrows originally performed the song "I Love Rock and Roll" before Joan Jett made it famous.

836. Keith Richards of The Rolling Stones was arrested in 1977 for heroin possession. As part of his sentence, he had to play two shows for blind children in Toronto, Canada.

837. Neil Peart traveled to Rush concerts on his BMW motorcycle.

838. The only Beatle not inducted into The Rock and Roll Hall of Fame as a solo artist is Ringo Starr.

839. Bruce Springsteen's ancestors were among the first Dutch settlers in the New Netherland colony in the 1600s. The name "Springsteen" literally translates to "jumping stone".

840. The name Steely Dan is slang for a strap-on dildo.

841. AC/DC was inducted into the Rock and Roll Hall of Fame in 2003.

842. When Sex Pistols bassist Sid Vicious was on trial for the murder of his girlfriend, Nancy Spungen in 1978, Mick Jagger secretly paid Sid's legal fees.

843. Deep Purple's original name was Roundabout.

844. UFOs original name was Hocus Pocus.

845. The Stooges are credited with popularizing stage diving.

846. The Clash played their first gig opening for The Sex Pistols in Sheffield, England.

847. The Velvet Underground with Lou Reed served as the house band at Andy Warhol's studio in New York City.

848. Genesis was founded in Surrey, England.

849. Guitarist Joe Satriani sang background vocals on the hit song "Don't Dream It's Over" by Crowded House. He was friends with producer Mitchell Froom who produced the debut album by the band. Satriani also sang background on 7 other songs on the album.

850. The Rolling Stones' song "Midnight Rambler" is about Albert DeSalvo, the "Boston Strangler".

851. John Fogerty was once sued by his previous record company for plagiarizing himself. In 1970 Fogerty released "Run Through the Jungle" with Creedence Clearwater

Revival. In 1985 he released a solo song called "The Old Man Down the Road". Fantasy Records, who owned the copyright to "Run Through the Jungle" felt "Old Man" was just "Run Through the Jungle" with different lyrics. Fantasy Records lost the lawsuit.

852. After meeting Eric Clapton at a Miami Concert, Eric invited Duane Allman to play on his album "Layla".

853. Before playing full-time with Slayer, bassist Tom Araya was a respiratory therapist.

854. The Yardbirds produced 3 legendary guitarists: Jeff Beck, Jimmy Page and Eric Clapton.

855. Paul McCartney and The Wings produced music for the James Bond movie "Live and Let Die".

856. Creedence Clearwater Revival were originally called "The Golliwogs".

857. Meatloaf's real name is Michael Lee Aday.

858. In the 1970s, Peter Frampton set the all-time sales record for his live album "Frampton Comes Alive".

859. Janis Joplin, Jimi Hendrix, and Jim Morrison all died in 1970.

860. Death Angel's debut album "The Ultra-Violence" was recorded while everyone in the band was under 20 years old. Drummer Andy Galeon was just 14.

861. After being kicked out of Metallica, Dave Mustaine wrote the song "Megadeth" while riding the bus back home to California. The song was eventually renamed "Set the World Afire" and appeared on the band's third album, "So Far, So Good...So What!".

862. Three separate bands called "Slayer" released albums in 1983.

863. Ted Nugent called the Pantera cover of his song "Cat Scratch Fever", "too white".

864. The song "(Welcome Home) Sanitarium" by Metallica was inspired by the opening riff of the song "Rainbow Warrior" by the band Bleak House.

865. When Nicko McBrain joined Iron Maiden he had left the French metal band Trust. His replacement was Clive Burr who had just left Iron Maiden.

866. Ozzy Osbourne used to shave off the eyebrows of his bandmates in Black Sabbath when they were sleeping.

867. Pantera once partied with the Dallas Stars after they won the Stanley Cup. Things got a little out of hand and the 106 year old statue got a 3 inch dent in it.

868. In 2012, Metallica formed the independent record label Blackened Recordings and took full ownership of their albums and videos.

869. Kerry King of Slayer played the ending guitar solo on the song "Goddamn Electric" on Pantera's album "Reinventing the Steel".

870. Cannibal Corpse performed in the movie Ace Ventura – Pet Detective. Jim Carrey gets up on stage with the band and performs.

871. Brownsville Station originally released "Smoking in the Boy's Room" in 1972. Mötley Crüe covered it in 1985.

872. On November 13th, 2015, the band Eagles of Death Metal were onstage performing to a sold out crowd at the Bataclan theater in Paris, France when a group of terrorists stormed the theater with automatic rifles, grenades, and suicide vests. The massacre resulted in the death of 89 people, including the band's merchandise manager.

873. The song "Summer of '69" by Bryan Adams was written when his friend Brodie bet him that he couldn't write a song with the number 69 in the title.

874. The Strokes admitted to taking their "Last Nite" riff from Tom Petty's "American Girl". Petty acknowledged it but said it didn't bother him.

875. Travis Barker of Blink 182 used to drum for The Aquabats under the stage name "Baron Von Tito".

876. Before Third Man Records was founded, Jack White of The White Stripes was a furniture upholsterer and owned Third Man Upholstery in Detroit, Michigan.

877. When he is not playing drums for The Pixies, David Lovering is a professional magician.

878. Drummer David Eagle was performing with his band OHM (ex-Megadeth guitarist Chris Poland) at The Baked Potato in Studio City, California. He suffered a heart attack and was rushed to the hospital where he died on August 3rd, 2015. On May 21st, 2016, OHM was performing a benefit concert for David's son at The Baked Potato with ex-Megadeth drummer Nick Menza. David's son was filming the show when Nick suffered a massive heart attack and died immediately.

879. The band Greta Van Fleet got their name from an elderly woman in Frankenmuth, Michigan named Gretna Van Fleet. They asked her for permission before they dropped the "n" and adopted it as a band name.

880. The Jeff Beck Group and Iron Butterfly were scheduled to appear at Woodstock but neither showed. The Jeff Beck Group broke up right before and Iron Butterfly got stuck at LaGuardia Airport and could not find transportation to the show.

881. In 1942, columnist Maurie Orodenker started using the term "rock and roll" in Billboard magazine to refer to upbeat music.

882. "Light My Fire" by The Doors was written by guitarist Robbie Krieger. It was the first song he had ever written.

883. Ozzy Osbourne hired Randy Rhoads as his guitarist after only hearing him warm up for his audition.

884. Judas Priest drummer, Dave Holland was never a full member of the band, despite playing with them full-time from 1979-1889.

885. Roger Daltrey of The Who described playing Woodstock as "The worst gig ever". They performed at the festival from 5am to 6:05am.

886. Led Zeppelin, The Beatles, Jethro Tull, The Doors, The Moody Blues, Spirit, Joni Mitchell and Free were all invited to play Woodstock but declined.

887. In January 1962, The Beatles were rejected by Decca Records after a New Year's Eve audition because "bands with guitars are on their way out".

888. On Pink Floyd's "Dark Side of the Moon", the man saying, "There is no dark side of the moon…really", is Abbey Road Studios doorman Gerry O'Driscoll.

889. Black Sabbath's debut album was recorded in one day on October 16th, 1969 during a single 12-hour recording session.

890. Jimmy Page bought Boleskin House on the Southern bank of Loch Ness in the early 1970s, driven by his long interest in the work of Victorian occultist and magician of the black arts, Aleister Crowley, who lived there in the early 1900s.

891. Iron Maiden were the first metal band played on MTV.

892. The Beatles' "Sgt. Pepper's Lonely Hearts Club Band" and Pink Floyd's first album "The Piper at the Gates of Dawn", were recorded at the same time at Abbey Roads Studio in London, in 1967.

893. Jimi Hendrix only played guitar for 12 years before his passing on September 18th, 1970.

894. Spirit drummer, Ed Cassidy is listed in the Guiness Book of World Records as the "World's Oldest Rock and Roll Drummer". Born in 1923, Cassidy was already 44 when he joined Spirit in 1967 and was 20 years older than his bandmates.

895. The Stone Poneys' (featuring Linda Ronstadt) big hit "Different Drum" was written by Mike Nesmith of The Monkees to be played on the TV show but was turned down.

896. Voyager 1 and 2 launched into space by NASA carries gold disks that have "Satisfaction" by The Rolling Stones on them, among other artists.

897. Because The Beatles were banned in Russian, bootleg copies were imprinted onto used x-rays taken from hospital dumpsters. They were called "music on the bones".

898. At dinner parties, Tom Waits often plays a live album by France's premier mime artist, entitled "The Best of Marcel Marceau". It features 40 minutes of silence followed by two minutes of thunderous applause.

899. Robert Plant once used a copy of Led Zeppelin's first album as an I.D. In the early days of Led Zeppelin, Plant attempted to buy a shirt he liked in a market on London's Carnaby street. When he tried to pay with a check, he was asked for I.D., he returned to his car to get a copy of Led Zeppelin I.

900. Ten out of the fourteen songs that comprise The Beatles first album "Please Please Me", were recorded in a little over 12 hours. That is one song every 72 minutes.

901. Bob Dylan's father was a semi-professional baseball player. He gave it up after he contracted polio in his 20s. He later became a furniture salesman in Minnesota.

902. Between 1950 and 1954, Johnny Cash worked as a radio operator with the U.S. Air Force Security Service in Germany, intercepting Soviet Army transmissions. In his role, he was the first American to learn of Joseph Stalin's death.

903. The Beatles were originally supposed to voice the vultures in "The Jungle Book" but due to scheduling issues it never happened.

904. Keith Richards never got his blood replaced. He went to Sweden to get it purified.

905. In 1983, drummer Jim Gordon who co-wrote "Layla" with Eric Clapton and played on "You're So Vain" by Carly Simon and "Imagine" by John Lennon, stabbed, and bludgeoned his mother to death. He remains in a psychiatric prison, convinced his mother is still alive.

906. Actress MacKenzie Phillips from the TV show "One Day at a Time" is the daughter of Mama's and the Papa's singer, John Phillips. She admits that her and her father had an incestuous relationship that lasted 10 years.

907. Keith Moon of The Who ran over his chauffeur, killing him instantly.

908. Leslie West of Mountain had to have the lower half of his right leg amputated due to diabetes.

909. Jon Bon Jovi's parents suggested to Sebastian Bach at the wedding of photographer Mark Weiss, that he try out for their son Jon's friend, Dave Sabo's band, Skid Row.

910. Rob Zombie's parents worked for a carnival. They quit when a fire was set on one of the tents and a massive riot broke out.

911. Ozzy Osbourne guitarist, Zakk Wylde wanted a vertigo design painted on his Les Paul to differentiate his guitar from former Ozzy guitarist Randy Rhoads who was killed in a plane crash on March 19th, 1982 in Leesburg, Florida. However, his friend Max painted a bullseye design instead. Zakk had a photo shoot that day and did not have time to repaint it. So, the bullseye design stayed.

912. In 2015, the Porsche 365 Joplin bought in 1968 broke records when it sold at auction for $1.76 million. It was painted all over with a bright mural of birds, butterflies, floating eyes, landscapes, mushrooms, and skull-like faces. Typically, celebrity ownership does not increase a car's value by much. But this was an exception, and it was the highest price ever paid for any Porsche 356 at auction.

Rock and Roll Facts

913. The night of Jimi Hendrix's first gig in London, Jeff Beck was coming out of the club when he ran into Pete Townshend and Eric Clapton going in. Eric asked him "Is he that bad?", Beck replied "No. He's that good."

914. The three symbols on the cover of The Police's "Ghost in the Machine" are supposed to represent the band's three personalities.

915. Mitch Mitchell, the drummer for The Jimi Hendrix Experience, took his first drum lesson from amp maker Jim Marshall of Marshall Amps.

916. As a child, Keith Richards dressed in cowboy outfits, complete with holsters and said he wanted to be like Roy Rogers and play guitar.

917. Joe Perry once had his prized Les Paul guitar stolen. It ended up in a pawn shop and the dealer offered it to Slash who was a huge Aerosmith fan. Joe pleaded with Slash to buy it back, but he would not sell it to him. Slash surprised Perry with it at his 50th birthday party.

918. The Sex Pistols' manager Malcolm McLaren used to give them words that he wanted them to brainstorm and make songs from. One of these words was "submission". McLaren expected a song about handcuffs and sex, but the band gave him lyrics about a submarine mission.

Rock and Roll Facts

919. Nikki Sixx of Mötley Crüe was born in San Jose, California.

920. Guns N' Roses recorded the song "Patience" during an evening of drinking. The next morning, they listened to it and liked it but had to redo the vocals because they could hear singer Axl Rose vomiting.

921. One day before Tom Petty's death, he did an interview. The interviewer asked him how long he would play with the Heartbreakers, he replied "until one of us gets sick or passes away".

922. John Bonham of Led Zeppelin died of choking on his own vomit after too much drinking. Coincidentally, when he was born, the doctor that delivered him was drunk.

923. Led Zeppelin guitarist Jimmy Page plays guitar on the Stones hit "One Hit to The Body."

924. Since 1974, former Faces guitarist Ronnie Wood has handled the Stones' lead guitar work. Wood is also a critically acclaimed painter, whose art has been sold at the San Francisco Art Exchange.

925. Sha Na Na, the doo wop group performed right before Jimi Hendrix at Woodstock. They got the gig because Hendrix was a friend of theirs.

926. The reverse-echo effect on Led Zeppelin's "Whole Lotta Love" was due to track bleed-through that sound engineer Eddie Kramer could not get rid of and so, he added reverb to it.

927. Randy Meisner joined Poco as their bassist but left before their first album. He then joined The Eagles. Timothy B. Schmidt replaced him in Poco. Right before The Eagles recorded "Hotel California", Randy left to pursue a solo career and once again, Timothy B. Schmidt replaced him.

928. The money used to score the heroin that killed Sid Vicious was given to him by his mother, who was under the impression that he was going to use the money to buy cocaine.

929. Drummer Neil Peart of Rush wrote most of the lyrics for the band.

930. In 1968, LIFE Magazine called Jimi Hendrix "The most spectacular guitarist in the world".

931. Eddie and Alex Van Halen's father was a band leader. His clarinet work can be heard on the Van Halen song "Big Bad Bill".

932. In 1955, Elvis Presley was interviewed on Town and Country Time. He was so nervous that he answered every question with "yep" and "nope".

933. Studies have shown that listening to metal music reduces negative emotions. It can also reduce the levels of the stress hormone cortisol in the body.

934. Black Sabbath's debut album was recorded with almost no second-takes and no overdubs.

935. On April 18th, 1987, MTV aired Headbanger's Ball for the first time.

936. Before uniting with Public Enemy, Anthrax teamed up with hip hop group UTFO on the song "Lethal".

937. Jeff Scott Soto, singer for Yngwie Malmsteen recorded the soundtrack for early-90s cartoon, Biker Mice from Mars.

938. The singing voice of Mark Wahlberg in the movie "Rockstar" with Jennifer Aniston is that of Steelheart vocalist Miljenko Matijevic.

939. Chickenfoot was a true Supergroup. Consisting of Joe Satriani (guitar), Sammy Hagar (vocals), Michael Anthony (bass) and Chad Smith (drums).

940. KORN were the first white artists to perform at The Apollo Theater since Buddy Holly.

941. Slipknot refers to their fans as "maggots" because drummer Joey Jordison observed fans "feeding off the music".

942. Dave Grohl was once a "nameless ghoul" in the band Ghost where every member remains anonymous.

943. Ozzy Osbourne once set off fireworks in a hotel lobby and hotel room and caused more than $200,000 in damages.

944. Dave Mustaine of Megadeth breeds horses.

945. Eleven people were crushed to death as thousands of fans stormed the Riverfront Coliseum in Cincinnati to get into a Who concert on December 3rd, 1979. Afraid that canceling

the show would spark more chaos, the organizers did not tell the band about the tragedy until after the concert.

946. Billy Gibbons, Dusty Hill and Frank Beard of ZZ Top were all born in the same year: 1949.

947. Davey Jones of The Monkees, appeared on the Ed Sullivan Show the same night as The Beatles, 2 years prior to becoming a Monkee.

948. There was no official merchandise sold at Woodstock in 1969.

949. The original bassist of The Rolling Stones, Bill Wyman had once stated that he felt as if he was born to be a librarian. This is because he used to catalogue everything.

950. Elvis Presley, Chuck Berry, James Brown, Ray Charles, Sam Cooke, Fats Domino, The Everly Brothers, Buddy Holly, Little Richard, and Jerry Lee Lewis were the first inductees into The Rock and Roll Hall of Fame in 1986.

951. Pink Floyd got their name from Pink Anderson and Floyd Council, two blues musicians whose records were in Syd Barrett's collection.

952. The Doobie Brothers are from San Jose, California.

953. Steely Dan added a ninth to virtually every chord they played. They called this technique the MU CHORD.

954. The Rolling Stones played their first gig at London's Marquee Club on July 12, 1962.

955. The Sex Pistols rejected their 2006 induction into The Rock and Roll Hall of Fame. They issued a handwritten statement that said the museum was "urine in wine".

956. After Peter Frampton's career stalled, a former childhood friend at Bromley Technical High School in London helped him reclaim his career. His name was David Bowie and he invited Frampton to open his Glass Spider Tour.

957. Les Paul was Steve Miller's Godfather and taught him to play guitar.

958. When Tom Petty was 11 years old, he met Elvis Presley and it changed his life.

959. Jerry Garcia was not happy with his and the Grateful Dead's performance at Woodstock, calling it a "disappointment".

960. At a party held by producer Paul Rothchild, Janis Joplin rejected Jim Morrison's advances, but he persisted, until Joplin hit him over the head with a bottle of Southern Comfort.

961. David Lee Roth insured his sperm. The reason being, if he got a lot of groupies pregnant, it could bankrupt him. By purchasing an insurance policy on his sperm, he protected himself and his assets.

962. In 2008 Jimmy Page of Led Zeppelin reached out to Steven Tyler of Aerosmith to form a new band. The band would consist of Page, Tyler, John Paul Jones and John Bonham's son Jason Bonham. After they rehearsed, Tyler said he could tell it would not work.

963. The parents of Rush bassist/vocalist, Geddy Lee were holocaust survivors.

964. Joe Satriani played with Mick Jagger. During the audition, Mick wasn't there. When he walked in, Joe just kept playing and was not starstruck. Mick was impressed and hired Joe on the spot.

965. At 19, Steve Vai mailed Frank Zappa a complete transcription of Zappa's "The Black Page" along with a tape of his playing. He was then hired by Zappa to transcribe several of his songs, a job which later lead to Vai being invited to become a full member of the band.

966. Metallica has won more than 9 Grammy awards.

967. Axl Rose is an anagram for "oral sex".

968. London socialite Tara Browne is the inspiration behind The Beatles' "A Day in the Life".

969. Drummer Keith Moon's habit of blowing up toilets with fireworks led him to get banned from the Holiday Inn, Sheraton and Hilton chains for life.

970. The sounds you hear when you use Microsoft Vista are created by prog rock guitarist and King Crimson frontman, Robert Fripp.

971. Singer Screamin' Jay Hawkins fathered around 75 children.

972. The Ramones took their name from the pseudonym Paul McCartney used when checking into hotels when he was in The Beatles: Paul Ramone.

973. Brian Jones of The Rolling Stones played oboe on The Beatles' track "Baby You're a Rich Man".

974. On their infamous 1977 tour, Emerson, Lake and Palmer took along 63 roadies, a karate instructor a 70-piece orchestra and their own doctor. They also had a "carpet roadie" whose job was to transport and sweep the Persian rug Greg Lake stood on during the concerts.

975. Sex Pistol John Lydon and his wife Nora were scheduled to be on the doomed Lockerbie flight that was blown up by a terrorist bomb in 1988 but missed it because Nora hadn't packed in time. The Four Tops were also booked onto the flight but missed it after a recording session ran over.

976. Queen's multi-millionaire drummer Roger Taylor was once spotted in Guildford's Sainsbury's supermarket filling out a National Lottery ticket.

977. Metallica drummer Lars Ulrich is a modern art collector. In 2008 he auctioned his "last Basquiat" for $13.5 million.

978. Slash was born in Hampstead, London not Stoke, England.

979. U2 are not all Irish. Adam Clayton was born in Oxfordshire, England to English parents. The Edge (David Evans) was born in Barking, east London to Welsh parents.

980. May 15th is officially ZZ Top day in Texas.

981. Before Pearl Jam, Eddie Vedder was the singer in Bad Radio, a progressive funk rock band influenced by early Red Hot Chili Peppers.

982. Elvis Presley weighed 170lbs following his discharge from the US Army in 1960. When he died, in 1977, he weighed 260lbs.

983. Andy White, the drummer who played on the definitive version of The Beatles' Love Me Do, never earned more than his original session fee of £7 from the track.

984. Since their inception, Guns N' Roses have had 21 full-time band members and counting.

985. In his youth, Red Hot Chili Peppers frontman Anthony Kiedis's babysitters included Cher and Sonny Bono.

986. Acclaimed UK cook and author Delia Smith baked the cake on the cover of The Rolling Stones' 1969 masterpiece "Let It Bleed".

987. Hard rock production guru Brendan O'Brien (Soundgarden, AC/DC, Pearl Jam) plays Hammond organ on Bob Dylan's MTV Unplugged.

988. Tom Morello of Rage Against the Machine's father, Ngethe Njoroge, a Kenyan, was the country's first ambassador to the United Nations.

989. Edward Van Halen's middle name is Lodewijk, after composer Ludwig van Beethoven. (Lodewijk is the Dutch version of Ludwig.)

990. Steven Van Zandt (Bruce Springsteen, Silvio Dante in The Sopranos) wears a bandana to cover permanent loss of hair from a car accident, where he hit a windscreen with his head.

991. Red Hot Chili Pepper John Frusciante once planned to audition for Frank Zappa - until he found out about Zappa's strict 'no-drugs' rule for his band.

992. The Clash's original sticksman Terry Chimes was cured of 'serious arm pain' in 1985 by Black Sabbath's personal chiropractor. After touring with Sabbath in 1987/88, the drummer set up Chimes Chiropractic and has over 30,000 patients on file. They also do acupuncture.

993. Pink Floyd performed under various monikers in their early years, including Tea Set, Sigma 6, The Screaming Abdabs and Leonard's Lodgers (after their landlord Mike Leonard).

994. Pseudonyms used by Paul McCartney in his career include Paul Ramone, Bernard Webb, A Smith, Apollo C Vermouth, Country Hams, Percy 'Thrills' Thrillington... and, of course, The Fireman.

995. Keith Richards' preferred tipple is vodka (2 measures) with Sunkist orange soda (1 measure), plus ice. He calls this refreshing drink Nuclear Waste.

996. Kings of Leon's regular co-writer Angelo Petraglia has also written songs for country stars Martina McBride, Tim McGraw and Trisha Yearwood.

997. Lemmy of Motorhead's first band were called The Rockin' Vickers. They were the first British band to play behind the so-called 'Iron Curtain' when they visited Yugoslavia in 1965.

998. Orville Gibson, founder of The Gibson Guitar Corporation in Kalamazoo, Michigan in the late 1890s, only registered one design patent. It was for the first archtop mandolins he made.

999. Elvis Presley's house Graceland was named after original owner SE Toof's daughter, Grace. It is the second most visited private residence in the United States outside the White House.

1000. Before settling on ex-Scream member Dave Grohl, Nirvana went through five drummers: Aaron Burckhard (1987-1988), Dale Crover (1988 and 1990), Dave Foster (1988), Chad Channing (1988-1990) and Dan Peters (1990).

1001. AC/DC's Angus Young is 5'2" tall.

1002. In 2002 Mick Jagger was knighted. Keith Richards thought it was hypocritical.

1003. Pete Townshend is partially deaf. When The Who made an appearance on The Smothers Brothers Comedy Hour, drummer Keith Moon decided to put explosives in his drum kit. When the explosives went off, Townshend was standing next to the kit. The incident caused permanent damage and tinnitus in his ears.

1004. Allman Brother's guitarist Duane Allman died in a motorcycle crash in Macon, Georgia on October 29th, 1971 when his motorcycle hit the side of a flatbed truck. He was 24 years-old. On November 11th, 1972, Allman Brother's bassist Barry Oakley was riding his motorcycle when he crashed into a bus just three blocks away from where Duane Allman was killed. Oakley was also 24 years-old. They are buried next to each other at the Rose Hill Cemetery in Macon, Georgia.

1005. AC/DC vocalist, Brian Johnson was recommended to the band when a fan from Chicago, Illinois sent a letter to AC/DC's record company telling them they should hire the singer from the band Geordie. The label got in contact with Johnson but originally, he was not interested because the label personnel would not tell him who the band was. She finally gave in and said "I will give you their initials. It is AC and DC."

1006. Brian Jones, co-founder of The Rolling Stones, was proficient at over 60 instruments.

1007. Lynyrd Skynyrd's "Free Bird" is dedicated to Duane Allman of The Allman Brother's Band.

1008. The Muppet Show's "Animal" is inspired by Mick Fleetwood.

1009. Instrumental virtuoso guitarist Tony MacAlpine is also a virtuoso pianist who during his live performances will sometimes play guitar and piano at the same time.

1010. The Rolling Stones recorded "Nineteenth Nervous Breakdown" after Mick Jagger announced how exhausted he was after touring, "I don't know about you blokes, but I feel about ready for my 19th nervous breakdown."

1011. The Beatles' "White Album" was originally titled "A Doll's House".

1012. Bob Dylan's first draft of the song "Like a Rolling Stone" was six pages long.

1013. Ted Nugent has never taken drugs of any kind.

1014. In 2001, radio conglomerate Clear Channel Communications, the largest owner of radio stations in the United States, compiled an advisory list of songs which stations might wish to avoid playing in the short term following the terrorist attacks on The World Trade Center and The Pentagon. That list includes such classic rock standards as:

Steve Miller "Jet Airliner"
Van Halen "Jump"
Queen "Another One Bites the Dust"
Queen "Killer Queen"
Pat Benatar "Hit Me with Your Best Shot"
Kansas "Dust in the Wind"
Led Zeppelin "Stairway to Heaven"
The Beatles "A Day in the Life"
The Beatles "Lucy in the Sky with Diamonds"
The Beatles "Ticket To Ride"
The Beatles "Obla Di, Obla Da"
Bob Dylan "Knockin' on Heaven's Door"
Arthur Brown "Fire"
Paul McCartney and Wings "Live and Let Die"
Billy Joel "Only the Good Die Young"
Barry McGuire "Eve of Destruction"
Steam "Na Na Na Na Hey Hey"
Drifters "On Broadway"
Shelly Fabares "Johnny Angel"
Los Bravos "Black is Black"
Peter and Gordon "I Go To Pieces"
Peter and Gordon "A World Without Love"

Elvis "(You're the) Devil in Disguise"
Zombies "She's Not There"
Elton John "Benny & The Jets"
Elton John "Daniel"
Elton John "Rocket Man"
Jerry Lee Lewis "Great Balls of Fire"
Santana "Evil Ways"
Louis Armstrong "What A Wonderful World"
Youngbloods "Get Together"
Ad Libs "The Boy from New York City"
Peter Paul and Mary "Blowin' in the Wind"
Peter Paul and Mary "Leavin' on a Jet Plane"
Rolling Stones "Ruby Tuesday"
Simon And Garfunkel "Bridge Over Troubled Water"
Happenings "See You in September"
Carole King "I Feel the Earth Move"
Yager and Evans "In the Year 2525"
Norman Greenbaum "Spirit in the Sky"
Brooklyn Bridgevv "Worst That Could Happen"
Three Degrees "When Will I See You Again"
Cat Stevens "Peace Train"
Cat Stevens "Morning Has Broken"
Jan and Dean "Dead Man's Curve"
Martha & the Vandellas "Nowhere to Run"
Martha and the Vandellas/Van Halen "Dancing in the Streets"
Hollies "He Ain't Heavy, He's My Brother"
San Cooke / Herman Hermits, "Wonderful World"
Petula Clark "A Sign of the Times"
Don McLean "American Pie"
J. Frank Wilson "Last Kiss"
Buddy Holly and the Crickets "That'll Be the Day"
John Lennon "Imagine"
Bobby Darin "Mack the Knife"
Surfaris "Wipeout"
Blood Sweat and Tears "And When I Die"
Dave Clark Five "Bits and Pieces"
Tramps "Disco Inferno"
Paper Lace "The Night Chicago Died"

Frank Sinatra "New York, New York"
Creedence Clearwater Revival "Travelin' Band"
Neil Diamond "America"
Tom Petty "Free Fallin'"
Bruce Springsteen "I'm On Fire"
Bruce Springsteen "Goin' Down"
Phil Collins "In the Air Tonight"
Chi-Lites "Have You Seen Her"
Animals "We Gotta Get Out of This Place"
Fontella Bass "Rescue Me"
Mitch Ryder and the Detroit Wheels "Devil with the Blue Dress"
James Taylor "Fire and Rain"
Edwin Starr "War"
Lynyrd Skynyrd "Tuesday's Gone"

NOTES:

NOTES:

NOTES:

ABOUT THE AUTHOR

Bill Lonero is an accomplished musician with 4 albums to his credit. He has played with some of the biggest names in rock music. He is also the inventor/co-owner of a successful music product. When he isn't playing guitar, Bill can be found writing screenplays, writing music, working on books, practicing Combat Hapkido and Krav Maga, volunteering on the U.S.S. Hornet Aircraft Carrier, playing golf or shooting landscape photography.

Rock and Roll Facts. Copyright © 2020 Bill Lonero. All rights reserved. No part of this book may be copied or transmitted without the express written permission of the author.

Printed in Great Britain
by Amazon